SOUNDTRACK TO THE REVOLUTION

# SOUNDTRACK TO THE REVOLUTION

**Free Jazz and Leftist Nationalism in Quebec**
**1967-1975**

ERIC FILLION

TRANSLATED BY DAVID HOMEL

Véhicule Press

Published with the generous assistance of the Canada Council for the Arts and the Canada Book Fund of the Department of Canadian Heritage.

Canada Council for the Arts Conseil des arts du Canada

Canada

Cover design by David Drummond
Set in Minion and Gill Sans by Simon Garamond

Originally published as *JAZZ LIBRE et la révolution québécoise* by M Éditeur,


Dépôt légal, Library and Archives Canada and the Bibliothèque nationale du Québec, second trimester 2025

Library and Archives Canada Cataloguing in Publication

Title: Soundtrack to the revolution : free jazz and leftist nationalism in Quebec 1967-1975 / Eric Fillion ; translated by David Homel.
Other titles: Jazz libre et la révolution québécoise. English.
Names: Fillion, Eric, author. | Homel, David, translator.
Description: Translation of: Jazz libre et la révolution québécoise. | Includes bibliographical references and index. | Translated from the French.
Identifiers: Canadiana (print) 20250114372 | Canadiana (ebook) 20250115352 | ISBN 9781550656855 (softcover) | ISBN 9781550656886 (EPUB)
Subjects: LCSH: Quatuor de jazz libre du Québec. | LCSH: Quatuor du nouveau jazz libre du Québec. | LCSH: Jazz musicians—Québec (Province)—Biography. | LCSH: Free jazz—Québec (Province)—History and criticism.
Classification: LCC ML421.Q2 F4813 2025 | DDC 781.65/6—dc23

Published by Véhicule Press, Montréal, Québec, Canada
www.vehiculepress.com

Distribution in Canada by LitDistCo
www.litdistco.ca

Distribution in the US by Independent Publishers Group
www.ipgbook.com

Printed in Canada

# Contents

ACKNOWLEDGEMENTS 7

PREFACE 11

INTRODUCTION 15

CHAPTER 1
The New Canadian Free Jazz Quartet (1967–1968) 29

CHAPTER 2
A Detour via Rock Music (1968–1970) 57

CHAPTER 3
Countercultural Jazz Vibes (1968–1970) 83

CHAPTER 4
Free Improv for Communal Living (1970–1973) 107

CHAPTER 5
The Inevitable Coda (1973–1975) 136

CONCLUSION 159

PHOTOS AND ILLUSTRATIONS 169

NOTES 181

BIBLIOGRAPHY 203

INDEX 209

# Acknowledgements

A BOOK LIKE THIS ONE would have been impossible without the invaluable contributions of the musicians who shared their memories and archives of Jazz Libre. I want to mention Patrice Beckerich, Jacques Beaudoin, Jean Martineau, Jean-Guy Poirier, Guy Thouin, and Jacques Valois. *Soundtrack to the Revolution* is dedicated to them.

This work is also dedicated to the memory of Yves Bouliane, Tristan Honsinger, Mathieu Léger, and Cyril Lepage, whom I was fortunate to meet, interview, and be inspired by. They left behind a deep legacy for improvised music enthusiasts to build on.

I would also like to thank Yves Charbonneau's and Jean Préfontaine's relatives for giving their support to this project: Danielle Chalifoux, Nathalie Charbonneau, Diane Dupuis, Françoise Labonne, Ève Préfontaine, and Nathalie Préfontaine.

A number of protagonists of this story were close to the members of Jazz Libre without necessarily joining the group. I am grateful for the generosity with which these people agreed to journey into the past, bringing back enlightening details and surprising anecdotes: Lise Balcer, Walter Boudreau, Georges Casavant, Robert Charlebois, Fernand Dansereau, Jean Derome, Michel Di Torre, Raôul

Duguay, Fernand Foisy, Louise Forestier, Lucien Francoeur, Errol Gagné, Jean Gagné, Serge Gagné, Bernard Gagnon, Billy Georgette, Bryan Highbloom, Richard Lacroix, Barry Lazar, Mark Lazar, Jean Pierre Lefebvre, Robert M. Lepage, Michel Madore, Albert Mayr, Pierre Monat, Claudine Monfette, Paul Morin, Erica Pomerance, Michel Robidoux, Lise Rose, Iolande Cadron-Rossignol, and Peter Zin (alias Peter van Ginkel and Peter Bastiaan). Raymond Gervais and Yves Préfontaine are no longer with us, but their writings and the stories they shared with me resonate in the pages of this book. They are missed.

I also wish to acknowledge the contributions of the archivists who helped me find my way through the material they are charged with preserving at these institutions: Bibliothèque et Archives Nationales du Québec, Bibliothèque des Livres Rares et Collections Spéciales de l'Université de Montréal, Centre Gaston-Miron, Concordia University Library and Special Collections, Library and Archives Canada, National Film Board of Canada, Services des Archives et de Gestion des Documents de l'UQAM, Service de l'Accès et de la Protection de l'Information de la Sûreté du Québec, Service des Communications de la Confédération des Syndicats Nationaux, and Vidéographe.

My sincere thanks to M Éditeur, the original French publisher, and especially to its former director Richard Poulin, and Sébastien Rioux for their careful rereading of and thoughtful commentary on the manuscript I sent them in 2018. Jazz Libre could not have had a better partner in the preservation of its memory. Isabelle Le Bourdais and her group of colleagues have since taken the helm of M Éditeur, and I am appreciative of the support they have offered for this English-language version of *JAZZ LIBRE et la révolution québécoise.*

Working with Véhicule Press has been a real pleasure, and I am thrilled to see *Soundtrack to the Revolution* appear alongside the many great jazz-related titles that Simon Dardick and Nancy Marrelli have published over the years. I am, of course, indebted to David Homel for his terrific work on the translation of the book, not to mention his collegiality and good spirits. Thanks also to Chris Greencorn (for his work on the index) and Siddhesh Inamdar (for his copyediting).

A large number of friends, colleagues, accomplices, and mentors contributed to this project at various stages and in various ways. You are aware that this book would have been no more than a thought without your support and eagerness to discuss history, music, and politics. I offer you my enormous gratitude. A special shout out to Marc Chénard, Mario Gauthier, John Gilmore, David Lee, Dominic Marion, Mark Miller, Sean Mills, Éric Normand, and Désirée Rochat for helping me (both directly and indirectly) think through ways of improving the original manuscript and increasing its reach.

And Valérie, thank you for staying with me along this road and following it to its conclusion. We had so much more to explore together. We did. I love you. Always will.

# Preface

IF YOU ARE IN MONTREAL or Toronto (or any other Canadian city with a deeply entrenched improvised music scene), walk into a bookstore and look for the music section. You will likely find a stack of *Coda* issues on the floor or on the top shelf. Founded in 1958, the magazine has been the go-to reference for generations of jazz enthusiasts in this country. Find the July/August 1972 issue and open it to page 9. At the bottom, there is a review of the album that Quatuor de Jazz Libre du Québec (Jazz Libre for short) recorded in December of 1968. The session "seems to be a conscious striving on the part of technically adept musicians to put together a program of so-called 'avant garde' jazz," wrote John Norris. To his ears, "the experiment was a failure." He added more tellingly, "Certainly not one to have been preserved on disc for future generations."[1]

Not only was the album reissued several times in the 1970s but it also became a highly sought-after collector's item until it was pressed onto vinyl again by Return to Analog Records in 2018. This latest reissue followed my own efforts to call attention to Jazz Libre's experimentations. In 2010, I founded the non-profit archival record label Tenzier to help preserve the history of avant-garde music in Quebec. The second album I put out was a previously unavailable session that the quartet had recorded in 1973. Chris Kennedy, writing for *Musicworks*, noted that "the music never feels derivative" and that it "definitely inspires further investigation of a fruitful moment in Québécois free jazz."[2] *La Scena Musicale*'s Marc Chénard agreed, adding that the session "reveals an essential quality, namely, a sense of urgency all too rarely heard in today's music, jazz and beyond."[3] In the wake of this work, Mario Gauthier and Éric Normand dusted off and began digitizing more than fifty reel-to-reel tapes that revealed Jazz Libre live in action from 1971 to 1974. We worked together on a 4-CD box set that pianist Stuart Broomer, a contributor to *The WholeNote* and a former *Coda* editor, described as "providing context for the most radical Canadian-born jazz movement in history."[4]

Clearly, Jazz Libre's free jazz continued—or rather continues—to resonate beyond the 1970s, despite what Norris predicted. As for the story of the musicians who created this music, it had yet to be told when I began the research for *JAZZ LIBRE et la révolution québécoise* back in 2010. This English-language translation of the book allows me to continue sharing that story today against a backdrop of lingering social and political conflicts. *Soundtrack to the Revolution* takes a close look at an especially turbulent moment in Quebec history to show how collective improvisation inspired resistance and hope by fostering communication, collaboration, initiative, trust, and self-criticism—but also a disposition to take risks as well as a willingness to think creatively and make decisions on the spur of the moment. The book examines Jazz Libre's successes and failures, including the flawed metaphors around which the group developed parts of its leftist nationalist project, to help us think more broadly about the intersection of art, politics, and community. In tracing the paths followed by these experimentalists, *Soundtrack to the Revolution* invites reflection on the ability of improvised music to catalyze all kinds of evocative solidarities, perhaps even futures.

While I find Jazz Libre's free jazz deeply engaging, even intoxicating (many will find it difficult to listen to), my primary interest in this group of musicians lay in their attempts to transform Quebec society, even if only from its margins. In other words, I am drawn to what Ajay Heble, the founding director of the International Institute for Critical Studies in Improvisation, calls "the 'sonic symbolism' of dissonance," a term that speaks to the potential social impact of "innovative models of musical practice."[5] As I note in the conclusion, music can create spaces for learning how to live together and fight the reactionary tendencies that damage our social fabric. This is as true today as it was six—or even fifty-eight—years ago.

# Introduction

*I am a revolutionary first, a musician second. Instead of a machine gun, I have a trumpet. I preach freedom to people. I tell them, "Play* free, *like me."*[1]

–Yves Charbonneau

THAT WAS HOW Yves Charbonneau, the trumpet player in Jazz Libre, described his work in an interview with Jacques Larue-Langlois, a journalist for the daily newspaper *La Presse*, at the beginning of May 1969.[2] Charbonneau had just returned from Paris and a series of concerts at the Olympia, where he shared the stage with star singers Robert Charlebois and Louise Forestier. Jazz Libre had accompanied them since the very first version of *Osstidcho*, a musical revue, one year earlier. This iconoclastic show, a mix of monologues and music, did wonders for the careers of Charlebois and Forestier, but not just them. The stage performers Claudine Monfette, alias Mouffe, and Yvon Deschamps benefited from the exposure. Together, these artists infused new energy into French-language rock, and Quebec's artistic expression in general, by exploding the rules governing the performing arts. The members of Jazz Libre—Charbonneau, Jean Préfontaine on saxophone, Maurice Richard on bass, and Guy Thouin on drums—earned a good measure of fame thanks to their work on stage that continued beyond Montreal, then in the studio and on records. The group's incursion into showbiz, just like its foray into rock, did not last long, however. Leftist nationalism began to occupy its members by the end of the decade.

Charbonneau and the rest of the group were impatient with the politician class and what they saw as its unwillingness to act when it came to the issue of the national question in Quebec. Yet the province had made great progress, starting with premier Jean Lesage's groundbreaking program of reforms, spurred by the motto "Masters in our own House." The Liberal Party's rise to power in 1960 ended "La Grande Noirceur," the so-called reign of darkness associated with the previous premier, Maurice Duplessis, and his brand of reactionary conservative thinking. The years of the Quiet Revolution (1960–1966) were marked by a series of reforms that led to the modernization of Quebec society. Among them was the nationalization of certain sectors of the economy and the integration of the French language at all levels. As well, the state came to play a more active role in the social sphere; services were offered to the population outside of the framework of the Catholic Church; and the school system was revamped to help young French-speaking people play a greater part in the new Quebec society that was emerging. This sense of a definite break with the Duplessis era meant that the majority French-speaking population saw itself as now catching up with—and taking its rightful place within—Canada and the world. The country's largest city at the time, Montreal, was the hub of Quebec's move into the present. Re-elected mayor in 1960, Jean Drapeau carried out several large-scale projects, of which Expo 67 was the high point. This key event helped Quebec open up to the world by setting the province and its metropole at the centre of the celebrations around the hundredth birthday of the Canadian Confederation.

But not everyone saw things the same way. "Quebec IS a colony and the first thing to do is decolonize it," insisted Raoul Roy, the founder of the Association Socialiste pour l'Indépendance du Québec at the start of the decade.[3] André D'Allemagne, co-founder and first head of the Rassemblement pour l'Indépendance Nationale (RIN), was saying essentially the same thing when he stated that Quebec's colonial status was a result of francophones in North America being forced to negotiate with British power from a position of weakness after the conquest of 1760 and again with the founding of Canada in 1867.[4] First launched in 1963, the magazine *Parti pris* (meaning, roughly, "side taken") adopted the theme of decolonization in its desire to promote a "free, secular, socialist state."[5] Meanwhile, the Front de Libération du Québec (FLQ), a decentralized network of terrorist cells, was setting off its first bombs aimed at symbols of English Canada. The "decolonizing socialism" of the *Parti pris* group postulated that "French Canadians" suffered double oppression (as a nation and as a social class) in several sectors (economic, political, and cultural) within Canada.[6] Jailed at the turn of 1967, the FLQ leader Pierre Vallières used the time inside to write an essay called *White Niggers of America*, in which he put forward the idea that the situation of the French-Canadian proletariat was analogous to that of other peoples under the yoke of British and American imperialism. True revolution would be national and socialist, so he maintained. Published in 1968 (the English version appeared in 1971), this "precocious autobiography of a Quebec 'terrorist'" added new energy to independence-minded nationalists in the wake of Canada's centenary.[7]

This consequential work influenced Jazz Libre to put its music, a free jazz style borrowed from the United States, at the service of Quebec's revolution in the making. The group moved to Sainte-Anne-de-la-Rochelle in the Eastern Townships to set up a commune on a farm that had once been used as a hideout by members of the FLQ. The Petit Québec Libre (the name given to this utopian project that imagined itself the microcosm of a future "larger, free, socialist Quebec") was a place of communication, organization, and participation where militants from a variety of horizons could come together.[8] Young people from the counterculture and working-class families were most welcome, since Jazz Libre wanted this daring initiative—as improvised as its music was—to be a vector of collective awareness, the first steps toward the true liberation of the Quebec nation. By its very existence, the initiative would bring together movements opposed to power and participate in a common front between local organizations and revolutionary factions from the United States. The next step was inevitable. The members of the Petit Québec Libre commune, led by Préfontaine and Charbonneau, soon found themselves under Royal Canadian Mounted Police (RCMP) surveillance at a time when the federal agency was doing all it could to stop terrorist threats emerging from Quebec.

The free jazz that Jazz Libre took its inspiration from came mostly from two large cities in the United States: Chicago and New York. Through the 1960s, the music's ambassadors (Albert Ayler, Ornette Coleman, Cecil Taylor, Sunny Murray, and Archie Shepp, to name a few) adopted a combative stance by rejecting all stylistic conventions to experiment with form, instrumentation, and sound. Having eliminated the dictatorship of tempo and harmonic progression, they set down an innovative musical language based on collective improvisation, through which all the musicians, including members of the rhythm section, could express themselves freely. They created a new brand of music, often strident and challenging, unconcerned with the expectations of critics, record companies, and the entertainment industry. "New thing," "experimental jazz," and "anti-jazz" were just a few of the terms used to define this avant-garde music completely in touch with the unprecedented mobilization of the African diaspora in the United States.

In what ways was free jazz revolutionary? First, the exploratory style of the artists mentioned transgressed the framework used by the industry to circumscribe jazz and exploit its commercial potential, in many cases, at the expense of its African American musicians. Their free jazz displayed a desire to break with established order and the subservience it brought. Dissonant, the music was hard to co-opt. Multiple and polymorphous, it was hard to pin down, since no rules governed its creation, which meant that musicians could work together and push the limits of their research, sometimes to diametrically opposed horizons. This exploration offered, among other things, a new reading of the origins of jazz, including the transatlantic connections that linked it to African music and even to the Middle East. Free jazz mobilized people; it resisted cultural domination and refused assimilation into white America. The music's ambassadors called for historical awareness based on collective affirmation, just as a number of their compatriots in different organizations across the political spectrum were doing, from the civil rights movement in general to the National Association for the Advancement of Colored People to the Nation of Islam and the Black Panther Party. Of course, not all musicians were politically engaged, but the tendency (or the perception of it) was far-reaching enough to make free jazz the symbolic sound of Black revolt.

The first to theorize about free jazz maintained that the music could not be disassociated from Black nationalism or the international context of anti-colonial struggles. To their ears, it was the soundtrack of popular resistance to racial segregation and the institutionalized racism that informed life in the United States after the Second World War. Writer and activist LeRoi Jones (who later became Amiri Baraka) asserted in 1963 that this music stood for the radicalization of relations between the African diaspora and white America.[9] Frank Kofsky, Marxist historian and chronicler of jazz, agreed when he wrote that the musical movement constituted "a vote of 'no-confidence' in Western civilization and the American dream."[10] In a 1967 interview, Archie Shepp told him, "We are only an extension of that entire civil rights—Black Muslims—black nationalist movement that is taking place in America."[11] Meanwhile, French critic Jean-Louis Comolli was stating in 1966 that free jazz was much more than an engine of revolt against white America; it was the sound of the international fight against imperialism and capitalism. In his opinion, the music emerged from a proletarian consciousness, since it rejected capitalism and the normative structures of bourgeois aesthetics that Western colonialism had disseminated.[12] These theories were not necessarily supported by critics who were evaluating free jazz in strictly musical terms. Yet they were still valid for people whose political thinking predisposed them to a certain informed attention when listening to collective musical improvisation.

That was the case with Patrick Straram, a French expatriate in Montreal, a Marxist-Leninist sympathizer with ties to the situationists, who saw in free jazz a way of revitalizing the revolutionary energies of the left-wing independence movement in Quebec. Echoing Comolli, Straram wrote in *Parti pris* that the music was a means of liberation created by a collectivity searching for a practice both anti-capitalist and anti-imperialist; he saw his own community, the French Canadians among whom he now lived, as a colonized nation too. He called for a "necessary appropriation" of the music, convinced that they, as a francophone minority in North America, were well positioned to be moved by its rebellious power.[13] He believed that promoting the music was a way to bring the colonized French Canadian—as described by Vallières—to the status of a revolutionary thinker by building bonds of solidarity with his African American counterpart. For Straram, free jazz was an "everyday revolutionary practice"—liberation music that could create awareness and a desire for action as much for musicians as for members of the public.[14] He stated that "one of the guerilla actions we must launch now [...] is to begin the work of educating each Quebecker about jazz."[15]

Jazz Libre and Straram became unexpected allies in

this project. The group's move toward social action and political militancy was not unexpected, since they had experimented along those lines through new experiences in communication. Founded during the summer of 1967, the band set out to explore novel musical approaches in hopes of echoing the changes occurring in Quebec. Its members wanted to speak up in a new way. "We wanted to go beyond the borders of traditional jazz and ambient music—and by that, I mean the folk music of the *chansonniers* we were hearing on the radio—and explore new means of expressing ourselves," Thouin remembers.[16] He and his bandmates first heard free jazz on records and in Montreal clubs. The group then decided to abandon the cabarets and dance halls where they had been playing and start their own musical explorations. "The experiments we are trying out are musical, first and foremost," Préfontaine explained in January 1968.[17] The four musicians' creative process led them to abandon all structures and figurative representations to leave the way open for visceral expression tempered by the relationships between the players. Improvisation—built as it is on communication and self-criticism—was, for them, a method of reducing cultural alienation through the reconciliation of individual and collective voices.

As well as gaining experience in communication, Jazz Libre also learned more about new organizational methods through collective improvisation. The group was becoming increasingly aware of the social importance of its music as a way of bringing people together in a spirit of participation, both democratic and liberating. It turned toward cultural animation, a form of public performance aimed at empowering communities, to encourage its audiences to experience similar revelations. Working in a politically charged context, the group quickly established a connection between what it was doing and the leftist independence movements at the end of the 1960s. As we will see, Jazz Libre's move through the margins of the Montreal jazz scene led Préfontaine and his bandmates to meet *Parti pris* and FLQ members as well as militants from student and worker organizations. These encounters, as well as the books the group read (Marx's *Capital*, Mao Zedong's *Little Red Book*, and Vallières's autobiography) were crucial.

Without adhering firmly to any one particular ideology, Jazz Libre did come to believe that Quebec was a colony in need of liberation from British power. Its music was perfectly suited to become the soundtrack for the leftist nationalist revolution, since it echoed the struggles of the African diaspora in the United States. Most of all, it served as a way to lead people to communicate and make them aware of their ability to act for their own liberation. Préfontaine, in his efforts to explain the group's work, asked a number of questions:

> Is it a coincidence that the first Canadian group and, to our knowledge, the first group of "Whites" truly involved in free jazz, is made up of French Canadians, separatists, with socialist tendencies more or less radical depending on the individuals [?] Hasn't there been talk of the "white niggers" of North America and "*québécitude*?"[18]

This metaphor is paradoxical and problematic, even if it was used in a political and historical context where the concept of "race" sometimes served to distinguish "French Canadians" from "English Canadians," and where "Black" referred in some cases to a political rather than a racial identity, especially within certain internationalist networks that sought to create an Afro-Asian anti-imperialist front. Inadmissible today, it was used to legitimize both the left-wing independence movement in Quebec and the appropriation of free jazz in the 1960s there.

During its eight years of existence, Jazz Libre did all it could to define its approach and broaden its networks so that its *musique-action*, or music action, a musical-political praxis, would serve the cause of a French-speaking, socialist, independent Quebec.[19] Its many initiatives (concert forums aimed at students and workers, the self-governing arts summer camp it set up in Val-David, north of Montreal, the socialist commune it established in the Eastern Townships as well as its experimental cultural centre in Old Montreal) were all oriented toward the convergence of protest movements shaking Quebec. The group's fate was, as a result, tied to the leftist independence movement, a hodgepodge of groups in search of possible futures at the end of the 1960s and the beginning of the 1970s.

***

Writing the history of Jazz Libre is an opportunity to underscore the important role of cultural workers—individuals, groups, and their networks—in the left-wing independence project of the time. This story shines a necessary light on the cultural aspect of the work accomplished by militants who were challenging "the empire within" in Quebec.[20] It is also an original contribution to historiography, since these protagonists and their actions are often not included in studies concerning the 1960s and 1970s. In this book, I also take a new look at the continuities before and after the Quiet Revolution, from the revolt of the Automatists to the apolitical tendencies of counterculture youth, pausing to consider the political dissidence of many artists and performers as well as the situationism of some groups and the decolonizing socialism of others. These connections help us analyze the practices and discourse promoted by Jazz Libre in its quest for a revolutionary praxis. And they provide us with structure to rethink the history of the leftist independence movement from the point of view of its cultural production, especially Jazz Libre's music action between 1967 and 1975.

This history of Jazz Libre presents a wider analysis of the role played by free jazz in resistance movements. It allows us to consider this music as a universal practice without necessarily neglecting how it originated among—and helped mobilize—the African diaspora in the United States. In that way, *Soundtrack to the Revolution* is part of a body of work investigating the rapid growth and mutations of jazz beyond the borders of the United States. Some works turn away from issues relevant to racialized identities, better to insist on the universal character of jazz and the ability of European artists to give it an orientation both distinct and authentic. The story of Jazz Libre shows that free jazz can find its way through foreign social structures without losing any of the political and cultural urgency that inspired it. This book adds to other studies on jazz in Canada by positioning this music alongside rock and folk in the turbulent 1960s and 1970s, and also by taking on the relation between politics and music making, especially in the theatre of French-speaking Montreal at a time of international confrontation with capitalism and imperialism.

Jazz Libre's music action is a choice field of study for anyone wishing to pursue the work begun elsewhere of studying the social impact of improvisation in music as well as the primordial importance of collective groups (these often disappear behind the all but exclusive attention paid to the big names in the jazz pantheon). For the past several years, a number of researchers have begun a critical analysis of aesthetic borders, pushing them outward and considering the social and political dimensions of cultural phenomena. Their projects are working to understand the processes by which improvisation allows individuals to imagine new ways of being in—and creating relationships with—the world, in order to face their own differences and build communities together. In the chapters that follow, I explore the idea of improvisation as a social practice, taking the example of Jazz Libre, a collective that distinguished itself through its will to go beyond the usual jazz vocabulary and venues to interact not only with other musicians but with students and workers as well.

This book's point of departure is my interest in Jazz Libre's sound archives and the need to situate them—from an ethno-musical and historical perspective—in their social context. Rather than seeing Jazz Libre's *practice* as issuing from a *discourse* in response to an immutable *structure*, be it political, economic, or cultural, the analysis I am proposing will consider how these three components influenced each other and necessarily coloured Quebec's soundscape in the wake of the Quiet Revolution. This study is based on a multitude of textual and iconographic archives (such as posters, contracts, correspondence, administrative documents, personal notes, photos, investigative reports, tracts, and more), films and videos that help us see and hear Jazz Libre, reel-to-reel tapes that hold dozens of hours of previously unpublished recordings of concerts and discussions with the public, not to mention the interviews that I conducted with former members and associates of the group.

A book about Jazz Libre is in part an answer to Yves Robillard and his collaborators' wish when they wrote in the *Québec underground* anthology:

> One day we will have to recognize the importance of their contribution. Through their professionalism, continuity over the years, and the idealism that fuelled the members of [Jazz Libre], they gave and continue to give faith and trust to everyone who believes that the freedom of the imagination should be played out in the open. The group stands for the moral assertion of this ideal.[21]

The history that follows takes place in several settings used by Jazz Libre in its quest for a revolutionary practice. We will travel from its beginnings at the downtown Jazz Workshop to L'Amorce in Old Montreal via the Association Espagnole, the Colonie Artistique de Val-David, and the Petit Québec Libre. Charbonneau and Préfontaine made up the core of the group, even as several members came and went between 1967 and 1975. They are given an important place here, even as I try to escape the codes of biography to bring forth the collective dimension of Jazz Libre's point of view and work.[22]

*Soundtrack to the Revolution* intends to be a "popular" history in the way Préfontaine and Charbonneau used the word when they improvised in front of an audience: they were playing for both those in the know and those who had never heard such sounds before. Overall, this history moves chronologically as it follows the two musicians and their bandmates along their journey. The voices of the many musicians who moved Jazz Libre forward will echo through these pages, making the internal dynamics visible, if not audible. We will learn about the tensions that existed at the heart of the group between the two men who carried the revolutionary flame and their many associates, not all of whom believed in the leftist independence movement. What improvisation accomplished was this: except for rare occasions, Préfontaine and Charbonneau managed to build upon these tensions when they played together.

The chapters you are about to read follow the two musicians and their fellow players. I first discuss the genesis of Jazz Libre and the space they managed to make for themselves in the margins of the Montreal jazz scene (1967–1968). I accompany them on their brief incursion into showbiz and their immersion in Quebec's counterculture (1968–1970), then their move toward cultural animation (1968–1970 as well), and their revolutionary work with Petit Québec Libre (1970–1972). In the final chapter, I re-trace their efforts to give their music action new life within revolutionary politics divided by the need to choose between nationalism and socialism (1972–1975).

[1]

# The New Canadian Free Jazz Quartet (1967–1968)

*A made-in-Quebec jazz bomb that will explode all musical structure: the New Canadian Free Jazz Quartet.*[1]
–Emmanuel Cocke

JEAN PRÉFONTAINE, Yves Charbonneau, Guy Thouin, and Maurice Richard had their baptism by fire on September 12, 1967, as part of the Jazz Workshop, a series of concerts staged by a young promoter named Mike Armstrong at a club called The Barrel, at 1191 de la Montagne Street in downtown Montreal. The four local musicians had seen and heard the pioneers of free jazz at this venue: sax players Archie Shepp and Albert Ayler as well as drummer Sunny Murray, among others. The quartet of Montreal improvisers aspired to be the voice of this new music in Quebec as they took to the stage for a six-week engagement. The New Canadian Free Jazz Quartet—the name chosen by Armstrong to promote the group that had neither name nor leader—began its journey in the stifling heat of a cramped basement. The members quickly appropriated and translated the name they were given: they became "Quatuor du Nouveau Jazz Libre du Québec." Préfontaine and his group created enough interest to occupy the stage at the Jazz Workshop for the entire autumn of 1967. And then, on December 27, they began a second engagement that took them through the frigid Canadian winter.

Montreal journalists saluted the arrival of Quebec-made free jazz in this mythical avant-garde spot. "We're used to hearing New Yorkers at the 'Jazz Workshop' [...], so to see brothers, and good players as well, that does the heart good," wrote journalist and author Emmanuel Cocke.[2] Jacques Thériault said this in the newspaper *Le Devoir*: "This musical form is their daily bread. It could also become ours, if only for one long [...] night."[3] But Armstrong would put a stop to Jazz Libre's second stint, on January 18, 1968, for nebulous reasons. A disagreement over sharing the stage with a traditional American jazz ensemble may have been the impetus. Financial difficulties may also have explained the decision to break with the local musicians. The quartet, after enjoying the spotlight of the city's nightlife, suddenly found itself shut out of the space it had occupied for several months. The group was relegated to the margins of the Montreal jazz scene, where it soon discovered the role it was destined to play as the Quiet Revolution wound down. In this chapter, I will discuss their life in the margins.

## Prelude

The adventure of Jazz Libre begins with Préfontaine, the group's elder and the man everyone called "Doc," since he had studied medicine briefly at the beginning of the 1950s. He never earned a diploma, having decided to drop out of school to dedicate himself to music. He was born in Montreal, in 1926, in the relatively well-off Outremont district. During the Second World War, Préfontaine was in boarding school at the Séminaire de Joliette, outside of Montreal. He learned the rudiments of drumming as part of the student band, then turned to the clarinet and transverse flute. He soon began teaching himself tenor and alto saxophone; it looked less and less like he would follow in his biologist father's footsteps. Yet he did complete college and three years of medicine before starting a traditional jazz group in 1954. The next autumn, he joined the band of the Royal Canadian Ordnance Corps as a bassoon player. His time spent in the Canadian military did not stop him from dreaming of becoming a professional musician. He directed his own group and would accompany others on the cabaret stages of Casino Bellevue, the El Mocambo, Chez Parée, and the El Morocco.

Préfontaine was also deeply interested in the visual arts scene. There, too, voices were calling for a revolt against the traditionalism of the Duplessis regime. Doc was especially attentive to the subversive work of the Automatists who rallied around painter Paul-Émile Borduas. In their creations—spontaneous, intuitive, abstract—the young jazzman saw parallels with musical improvisation. Published in 1948, the Automatists' *Refus global* (*Total Refusal*) is one of the crucial junctures in Quebec's move toward modernity.[4] Though it expressed the need to break with traditional French Canadian society and its dogmas and values oriented toward the past, the manifesto was happy to "condemn society such as it exists," yet it neglected to show a way "towards political action to replace it and create conditions essential for the art to be independent."[5] All the same, *Total Refusal* and its signatories inspired more than a few people to try their hand at the creative arts as the 1950s began.

Préfontaine was one of them. He is of the same generation as painter Jean-Paul Riopelle, dancer and choreographer Françoise Sullivan, and poet Claude Gauvreau, three of the group who signed the manifesto. Doc gravitated around this artistic movement without joining it; he preferred the observer's position during that period. In May 1957, he married painter Marcella Maltais. At the time, she was preparing the show that would confirm her importance in the post-Automatist current. Together, they settled in France, and Préfontaine began studying music at the Paris Conservatory. Though the sojourn was valuable, Doc decided to put an end to his Paris days in the spring of 1959 and return to the Montreal jazz scene. Maltais stayed on in Europe, and the couple separated. Préfontaine's experiences in the world of the Automatists no doubt inspired him to move toward further explorations, even if he never did situate Jazz Libre in their lineage.

Born in 1940 in Montreal's gritty Centre-Sud neighbourhood, from boyhood, Thouin was determined to set himself apart from other rhythm section musicians. As a teenager, he tinkered with a banjo to turn it into a drum, then made himself an entire kit out of various percussion elements. He learned to keep time in a band that played at weddings, and took drumming classes to perfect the techniques he had learned on his own. He followed his father's example and finished his studies to become an optician, but chose artistic self-expression in the end. In 1963, he entered art school, where he studied sculpture and improved his knowledge of contemporary art. Two years later, he emerged with an increased receptivity to all forms of experimentation. That year, he joined singer

Pierre Nolès' *Clan de cuir*, a musical about young greasers in revolt; the show played across Quebec. The tour made it possible for him to take his drums on the road and break from the commercial music, including jazz, that he had been playing in clubs over the years. His time in art school left him with a clear need to rethink the way he played. Thouin's energy and swing greatly impressed Préfontaine, who was looking for musicians for a gig in Pointe-Calumet, a vacation and leisure spot at the mouth of the Lake of Two Mountains, north of Montreal.

Doc recruited Maurice Richard as well. He saw tremendous potential in him, even if the young bassist had very little experience with jazz. Born in the Saguenay region in 1946, Richard moved from one rhythm section to the next depending on what work was available. Like many players just starting out, he often worked for R&B and rock groups. Flexible by temperament and ready to compromise by nature, he agreed to experiment with jazz when Préfontaine and Thouin made him an offer in the summer of 1967. Music journalists in Montreal were hard on him when he started with Jazz Libre. They pointed out his amateur style and criticized his lack of involvement. "We'd like to see a little more participation from the bassist (when he's not playing, he leans heavily on his instrument), but the other three guys are good when it comes to creating an atmosphere."[6] That said, Richard did have the qualities needed to take his place in the quartet. He was curious and open-minded, which made it possible for him to venture into the terra incognita of collective improvisation.

The three musicians kicked off the summer at the Hôtel Pointe-Calumet, rounding out their quartet by drafting

Richard Chiasson, a young, multifaceted guitarist who was all but grabbed off the street for the occasion. The group's mandate was to get the vacationers onto the dance floor and accompany the various singers who took to the stage during the summer. But Préfontaine and Thouin were also eager to experiment with the new forms of jazz they had learned about that year. The fact that legendary pianist Thelonious Monk was playing at Expo 67 would have inspired them, but they had already discovered free jazz on the ESP-Disk label—a New York company known for giving its artists carte blanche to improvise. They heard many New York players at The Barrel, including drummers Rashied Ali and Sunny Murray. Only Thouin would find the time to jam with one of ESP-Disk's jazzmen. Late in the fall, just as Jazz Libre was picking up speed, he invited saxophonist Noah Howard to take a break from The Barrel and come rehearse with him as a duo. Though it did not last long, the experience convinced the young Quebec drummer that he had what it takes to pursue a career in free jazz.

The four players tried bravely to play this new music in Pointe-Calumet on Sunday afternoons. According to Préfontaine, the group offered "free jazz concerts that the customers appreciated."[7] In reality, the vacationers probably chose the beach over the quartet's tentative experimentation, especially if it was sunny outside. All the same, the summer of 1967 was a foundational season for Doc and Thouin. In Pointe-Calumet, a seed was sown: they might dedicate themselves entirely to collective improvisation. When the summer was over, they decided to bring their determination back to the Montreal scene. Only Richard accompanied them; Chiasson had other engagements for the coming year.[8]

Back in the city, the three musicians recruited a trumpeter they had met at The Barrel earlier in the summer. Born in working-class East End Montreal in 1934, Charbonneau had had enough, like his new colleagues, of getting dancers onto the floor and playing in traditional pop and jazz bands. He was passionate about Miles Davis's work and the experimental playing of Freddie Hubbard and Don Cherry. Married and the father of two, he was taking a risk by sacrificing his club musician's income to work with Préfontaine, Thouin, and Richard. This brand-new quartet was out to play music like the kind they had heard African Americans play at The Barrel that summer. They felt like they understood it completely. It was a sign of modernity, the sound equivalent of the creative revolt ushered in by the Automatists in the visual arts.

Right from the start, the four musicians chose to live together. They moved into the apartment that Thouin and his wife found on Papineau Street, near the former Au-Pied-du-Courant prison, where several rebels from the 1837 and 1838 uprising against the British colonial government were executed. They soundproofed the basement and turned it into their headquarters in September 1967. The free jazz they wanted to play involved creating collective expression from individual voices—which is why "we needed to live together to be able to communicate better personally and musically," Préfontaine explained.[9] According to Thouin, this proto-commune was not part of the counterculture movement of the times. He was opening his door to his colleagues to reduce the group's expenses and limit missed and late sessions during their daily rehearsals. The collective had no trouble with self-discipline; they were more like a commando unit. They let Armstrong know they were ready to be part of The Barrel's Jazz Workshop sessions. All they needed was a yes from the promoter and they would spring into action.

## Baptism by Fire

The group's brand of free jazz must have been persuasive, since Armstrong signed them on for a six-week engagement, from September 12 to November 26, 1967. There they were, in that mythical spot where they had first heard Shepp, Ayler, Murray, and other pioneers of that style earlier in the summer. At the time, Montreal was moving to the beat of Expo 67 and hosting most of the centennial celebrations. Armstrong offered a daring and original program, since he figured tourists would pour into the heart of the city on the weekends. As John Gilmore explains in his history of jazz in Montreal, The Barrel had not always been a welcoming place for lovers of avant-garde jazz:

> Armstrong had begun presenting jazz concerts the previous year at Moose Hall, better known during the late 1950s as the meeting place of the Traditional Jazz Club of Montreal, a group of fans and part-time musicians devoted to Dixieland and New Orleans-style jazz. Armstrong called his presentations the Jazz Workshop. [...] After a few concerts at Moose Hall, Armstrong moved to The Barrel, a [...] sort of folk and blues coffee-house during the evenings, but at midnight on Friday and Saturday nights Armstrong's Jazz Workshop took over.[10]

All through the fall and during part of the winter (from December 27, 1967, to January 18, 1968), Jazz Libre's mission was to dazzle the ears of anyone who dropped in on the workshop. It went about its work diligently and with great conviction, "in a tight rank, like an army on the march raising dust from a road."[11]

It is astonishing to see the enthusiasm that Jazz Libre created from the very start, considering how experimental its music was. The group did not present itself as explicitly political, which helped the media digest it. But it was definitely part of the trend toward modernity and openness to the world that followed Expo 67. During the winter of 1968, its members were interviewed on shows like *La Semaine des arts*, on the airwaves of Radio-Canada, and *Aujourd'hui*, on the French-language public television network. Articles in Montreal newspapers and magazines were quick to follow. A consensus was developing: Quebec-made free jazz was relevant. People were convinced that the quartet had the necessary vision to give body and soul to this music. Unafraid of hyperbole, Cocke exclaimed, "Their existence is miraculous and miracles only happen once."[12]

Despite such enthusiasm, some listeners were lending a more critical ear. Journalist Gilles Ouellet pointed out that "the cohesion and synchronization leave something to be desired," despite the sense of fraternity within Jazz Libre. He added, "Except when the rhythm is up-tempo, the ensemble gives the vague impression that its music is damped down, on the weak side, as if it hasn't yet found the right way to express itself, and is hesitating about how to do it." He did underscore Charbonneau's "very self-assured" technique as well as Thouin's prowess—"one of the rare drummers […] who can play a long solo without boring the audience."[13] Ouellet did go on to comment on the boldness, rigour, and inventiveness that Jazz Libre put into its music. Like others, he believed the group was headed for a promising, even international career. "Surely, they'll go far," Cocke prophesied.[14]

The members of Jazz Libre were not the first Montreal players to experiment with new forms of jazz. Among those who preceded them was Herbie Spanier, a trumpeter from Saskatchewan who lived in Montreal off and on during the 1950s and 1960s. His free, inspired style aligned with that of Ornette Coleman, whom he met in 1958. He was in California at the time when Paul Bley was living and working there. The Montreal-born pianist was leading a band that included Coleman and Cherry. For some time, Bley had been shuttling between Quebec, New York, and California. He occasionally returned north after settling down for good in the United States. On one occasion, he worked with René Thomas. Belgium-born, exceptionally talented, Thomas first came to Montreal in 1956. Like Bley, he had good relations with African American jazz musicians, and even rubbed shoulders with Davis and accompanied Sonny Rollins on record. Sonny Greenwich, a guitarist from Ontario, also travelled to Montreal, where he joined Sun Ra and his band when they played there in 1961. He would move to the city five years later. Many other improvisers could be added to the list, players who pushed the limits of jazz. They did not necessarily promote free jazz since the Montreal scene remained "faithful to music based on harmonic structures and clear rhythm sections," despite the abundance of encounters that created new ideas and repertoires.[15]

These jazzmen did not reject the generation before them. Their trios and quartets were perched on the borders of bebop, the music born during the 1940s that featured dizzying improvisation backed by complex harmonic structures and energetic rhythms. Small groups were springing up everywhere in the Montreal of the 1960s. Inevitably, they would share the spotlight with Lee Gagnon and Vic Vogel's big bands, faithful defenders of commercial music that had its roots in 1930s swing, as well as other groups, more or less big, and more or less mainstream. They featured virtuoso soloists revisiting and reviving standards that were popular among audiences and critics alike.

These musicians were building on the foundations set down by the city's Black community, starting in the 1920s. Though this heritage was insufficiently acknowledged at the time, it created the dynamics of the Montreal jazz scene. Settling in the Little Burgundy district north of the Lachine Canal, the community sprung up around the Canadian Pacific Railroad. A number of individuals worked for the company as porters. This was the case of Oscar Peterson's father. Rufus Nathaniel Rockhead, an immigrant from the Caribbean, also worked for the railroad before he invested his savings in a building at the corner of Mountain and Saint-Antoine Streets. Opened in 1928, Rockhead's Mountain Tavern (renamed Rockhead's Paradise a few years later) would be one of many venues to feature jazz, contributing to the neighbourhood's reputation as the "Harlem of the North."

Jazz-loving entrepreneurs and Little Burgundy musicians were quick to organize. They fought racism in the musicians' guilds and more established clubs. Working conditions improved during the 1940s thanks to the prosperity that resulted from the war effort. The enthusiasm that greeted trumpeter Louis Metcalf's International Band proved that audiences were ready to discuss civil and human rights issues. Born in Missouri, Metcalf moved to Montreal in 1946 to play bebop with his seven-member group who came from diverse ethnic origins. Using improvisation, he created bonds between his colleagues and showed audiences that his music promoted communication and even reconciliation between people. The idea that jazz had a social role would have a long way to go, but the seeds were sown and others would move in that direction.

At the end of the 1960s, the Montreal jazz scene was at a crossroads. Spared American prohibition that began after the First World War and ran until President Franklin D. Roosevelt put a stop to it in 1933, the city was a focal point of organized crime. It was easy to find nightclubs where gambling, prostitution, and other illicit activities were happening. In many of these places, jazz provided the soundtrack. Everything collapsed before Expo 67 when Mayor Jean Drapeau decided to clean up the city's image by declaring war on what he called "vice" as well as on the corruption that had allowed organized crime to flourish. His "clean-up campaign" was a blow to the nightlife that had made the city Canada's jazz mecca. Opening hours were cut back and alcohol licences made harder to obtain.

The attack on organized crime shook the foundations of clubs and the promoters who depended on their activities; the jazz scene was simply collateral damage. The advent of television and young people falling in love with a new disruptive sound called rock and roll also contributed to the downfall of live shows. Though a few groups took advantage of the employment offered by Expo 67, most musicians made only crumbs off the supposed windfall generated by the event. The conjuncture looked unfavourable, and a number of players moved into radio and TV studios, where work awaited those who knew how to transcribe music and read scores. No doubt about it: the context was less propitious for experimentation at the end of the 1960s.

The musicians from Jazz Libre stood apart in this soundscape through their negation of traditional jazz. The group tended toward atonal and polyrhythmic music with no clear structures and harmonic progressions, casting its members and their audiences into a void that they had to fathom and fill. Ouellet remarked humorously, "It is a welcome change from Lee Gagnon's marshmallow-flavoured cotton candy."[16] He also rightfully pointed out that Préfontaine and his gang were not the only ones in Quebec venturing into free jazz in 1967. One ensemble in particular was competing with Jazz Libre, and it was composed of Walter Boudreau's players.

Born in Sorel on the Saint Lawrence River, Boudreau came to Montreal in 1966 to study science at university, but he gave up that ambition to turn to music. He learned piano, then switched to the sax at age thirteen. He put together a pop group, then moved into jazz and composition. He was only nineteen when he burned up the stage at the Youth Pavilion at Expo 67. With Jacques Valois on bass and Richard Provençal on drums, and occasionally Pierre Leduc on piano, he launched into serious explorations of what avant-garde jazz could do. Boudreau stated that only this music "leaves us room so we don't get restricted to one aesthetic that will end up passé in a very short time."[17] He would later call his jazzman's journey an experience "that was very short, very intense, and enormously beneficial," since it led him to even broader musical forms.[18]

Boudreau refused to get stuck with a conservative community of musicians. The "very structured" and "very ordinary" style of jazz of his peers ran counter to his taste for experimentation. Of curious mind, he ended up at The Barrel, where he met Préfontaine and his group—"terrorists with instruments" driven by a desire "to avoid all possible clichés." The quartet's collective improvisation held a whole field of possibilities that Boudreau was eager to explore. Often, he would show up at the Jazz Workshop late in the evening, after finishing a concert elsewhere in town, and sit in with Jazz Libre. The young saxman had "transcendental experiences" of rare intensity.[19] These impromptu sessions were an important part of his musical development. They oriented his explorations and paved the way for the musical collaboration that would follow later, between 1968 and 1970. Yet Boudreau realized that his journey with Jazz Libre had its limits, since he was interested in free jazz above all "for aesthetic and sentimental reasons."[20]

The main characteristic of the quartet—and what separated it from Boudreau and other jazzmen mentioned in these pages—was its political thinking and involvement. After several months of collective improvisation and life in a proto-commune, the group's members took note of the inevitable rapprochement between their desire for musical liberation and their hopes of seeing Quebec become an independent country. Just as Jazz Libre was being shut out of The Barrel, Préfontaine declared that he and his colleagues had no other choice, as *indépendantistes*, than to work for freedom "in all possible forms."[21] Inspired by the affirmative tone of the African American musicians he discovered at The Barrel, the elder statesman of the group stated that "you need to be in rebellion to play that 'New Thing' the way you should." That was why, he said, "French Canadians, the white niggers of America, have [...] such a gift for jazz."[22] Préfontaine established the way that Jazz Libre would appropriate the music. In his way of thinking, in Quebec as in the United States, it was the instrument that would take people from individual to collective liberation. It was music for action.

## The Politics of Listening

With that conclusion, Préfontaine joined the intellectuals and artists who believed that jazz could mobilize people politically. Among them was his younger brother Yves, a poet and jazzophile, known for his writings in the magazine *Liberté* and his Radio-Canada radio show, *Les Orphées noirs* ("Black Orpheuses"), during which he played jazz and featured writing by Black authors, as well as *Jazz-sortilège* ("Jazz Spell"), a weekly program. In 1961, Yves published a number of articles in which he introduced two terms that anticipated the concept of music action: "biojazz" and "musicojazz."[23] The first referred to the idea that bebop incarnated the revolt of artists who, on a daily basis, faced discrimination from white America. The second put the prefix "musico" in front of "jazz" to show that the latter was a kind of action, not just a form of entertainment. "At the heart of what current jazz has to offer, its authenticity and involvement, there is also something new: rebellion, and a spirit of affirmation."[24] Doc's brother did not develop this argument further, but his comment shows the receptivity toward new forms of the music in Quebec as well as the need to understand their origins in order to better appropriate them.

A number of filmmakers chimed in by creating jazz-inspired works whose form and message pushed the idea that it was time to break with the established order. Examples include *Le chat dans le sac* (*The Cat in the Bag*, Gilles Groulx, 1964), one of the founding films of Quebec cinema and "a filmmaker's take on the concerns of certain groups of French-Canadian youth."[25] Claude, the main character of this feature-length film, wonders about his future. "Rebellious? Yes. Revolutionary? I don't know…"[26] He listens to jazz and reads Frantz Fanon's *The Wretched of the Earth* and Louis E. Lomax's *The Negro Revolt*. To hone his revolutionary thought, he consults *Parti pris*. An original soundtrack from John Coltrane's quartet accompanies him through the film. That same year, *L'homoman* (Jean Pierre Lefebvre, 1964), a short twenty-four-minute work about wandering and identity (its chapters deal with boredom, hope, travel, the madness of love, revolt, war, and the urge to go back to the land), featured original music by Stéphane Venne (in a trio with Michel Donato and Buddy Hampton). A poetic work inspired by surrealism, *La femme image* (Guy Borremans, 1960) and its soundtrack (René Thomas in a quartet with Bobby Jaspar, Freddy McHugh, and George Braxton) joined the fight against the political and cultural establishment. More than simple stylistic counterpoints, these soundtracks declared that jazz could have a mobilizing role to play in 1960s Quebec.

Patrick Straram supplied the theoretical foundation of Jazz Libre's music action. Straram was a French writer who settled in Montreal in 1958—a leftist jazzophile who had participated in the founding of the Centre de l'Art de l'Élysée and the magazine *Cahier pour un paysage à inventer*. The latter reflected his past membership in and ties to Letterist International and Situationist International. He published material by European colleagues (Asger Jorn and Ivan Chtcheglov) and put forward the idea that art has intrinsic meaning only in its oppositional relation to power:

> Poetry for its own sake, like any art form grasping for its own absolute, is simply a worthless piece of nothingness that cannot even hide its complicity with a state of fact. The state of fact against which every man must revolt to assume his human condition, and not make poetry the way others make chewing gum or an atomic bomb, or engage in white slavery or academic poetics.[27]

From his point of view, jazz was a true art form. It was the music of revolt, a means of expression for "a community that needed to invent one, in a context where the rule was for it not to express itself," as Straram said.[28]

An emblematic figure of Quebec's counterculture and left-wing independence movement, Straram sought to "awake people's consciousness" by establishing the link between jazz and politics.[29] He is the one who insisted most forcefully on the need to be receptive to this music and grasp its social power. His first important text on the subject appeared in the magazine *Liberté* in the spring of 1961. "Bluesologie" is a twenty-three-page exposition on the history of jazz, providing tools for his readers to come to understand the meaning of this "music of sensation *and* meditation, dialectic sound material that questions us as human beings, just as the time is ripe to do so."[30] He looked into the significance of improvised music, an act of communication both physical and spiritual, translating, through body and sound, the American experience. Jazz is "a collective art *and* an individual art," Straram explained.[31] He then added:

> In the 20th century, you can count on an art that lets people interpret their lives and interpret themselves to each other. In this century that subordinates people to scientific progress and the vagaries of History, jazz is a provocation. Jazz provokes because it is a living power. A few people are taking heed and living it.[32]

This universalist reading of jazz is close to that of the French writers and critics who inspired him at the beginning of the 1960s. Hardly surprising that he wrote the article in the weeks after he arrived in Montreal. The pieces he published in *Parti pris* starting in 1963 would mark a turning point in his engaged reception of the music.

We cannot overstate the importance of *Parti pris* for the Quebec leftist intellectuals and artists of those days. Its co-founders (André Brochu, Jean-Marc Piotte, Paul Chamberland, Pierre Maheu, and André Major) called for open discussion to demystify and dismantle the structures judged responsible for the province's cultural, economic, and political alienation. Their project aimed to go beyond—and not just catch up with—the present, and they took inspiration from the decolonial struggles that shook the Western world after the end of the Second World War. Marxism and its many variations, the existentialism of Jean-Paul Sartre, and decolonizing socialism were the three guideposts of *Parti pris*.

The *Parti pris* literary generation came together in the cafes and nightclubs of underground Montreal. It fed off jazz as it turned to "total refusal."[33] At first, it seemed to be following the path of the poets and writers of the beat generation, such as Jack Kerouac, Allen Ginsberg, and John Clellon Holmes, to name just three. That path was associated with bebop prose and spontaneous poetics inspired by the expressive forms of jazz.[34] But the co-founders of *Parti pris* were disinclined to subscribe to what they saw as an artists' revolt, jazzy or not. There are few references to beat-generation artists in the publication, except to mention the lifestyle they helped create. Chamberland called it an "individualistic revolt."[35] As for Major, he remembered the few Montreal beatniks who hung out in "cafés where jazz and poetry were a backdrop, a climate [...], an apprenticeship with its own rules like wearing a turtleneck and corduroy pants." "That kind of underground never went very far," he added.[36] Maheu did concede that the revolt had its reasons, and that sometimes it could lead to revolutionary consciousness. In his opinion, "some were beatniks and rebels, and others with their leather jackets and motorcycles were young delinquents." He went on to say, "The forms of this revolt varied according to the individual, but the way of acting was fundamentally the same. Everything was cause for opposition. To take the expression of a precursor, it was total refusal."[37]

The Automatists' revolt was not based on anything to do with jazz, at least not explicitly, despite the fact that the group preached free and spontaneous creativity. Their revolt was nonetheless important for Maheu and his colleagues. It validated the idea that *Parti pris* "was part of an ideological evolution that was intrinsically *québécoise*."[38] The revolt was necessary, said Maheu:

> The members of the *Total Refusal* group could not hope to transform society, but even without that hope, they crossed a great threshold. They created a fundamental dialectical turnaround: they demanded a new culture and declared war on the old one. They took us from the Hermit to the Rebel.[39]

Chamberland added that revolt is pre-political, and that, to go beyond, it must help reconcile individuals with the collectives they belong to. For him, that meant substituting lived life for the poetic universe in the hope of "demystifying alienated daily life" and contributing (by spontaneous writing analogous to jazz) to the emergence of a true "common consciousness."[40] As his confreres in *Parti pris* explained it, revolt will "foster revolutionary attitude."[41]

According to them, that path was bound to lead to an independent, secular, socialist Quebec. Among the *Parti pris* group, there was deep dissatisfaction with the reforms begun by the provincial government starting in 1960. They did not go fast enough or far enough when it came to ridding the social sphere of the Church and bringing in measures to combat American cultural imperialism and the English-speaking population's domination of the province's economy. In their 1965 manifesto, they wrote, "For the neo-bourgeoisie, peace and quiet is what's important. They have no interest in changing the system; their only interest is a change [...] in power-sharing among the dominant classes."[42] The magazine took up the theme of decolonialization used earlier by Raoul Roy to situate his idea of independence in the context of international struggles. The "decolonizing socialism" of the *Parti pris* group postulated that Quebeckers suffered from double oppression, a position of alienation determined by "internal (between classes) and external (between nations) antagonisms."[43] Quebec needed a revolutionary praxis that would be both anti-capitalist and anti-imperialist.

Straram maintained in *Parti pris* that jazz was just that praxis. He based his point of view on the writings of his situationist comrade Guy Debord and those of Marxist philosopher Henri Lefebvre. The latter was interested in the processes by which power relations that structure bourgeois societies are reproduced in daily life. He studied the notion of leisure and underscored the hold that the capitalist system has on all social space. "Leisure and work and private life constitute [...] a dialectic whole, a global structure," Lefebvre wrote, that alienates the individual and cuts off any escape.[44] He proposed a critique of everyday life that exposed the structures that govern and oppress social beings in all the moments of their existence. The critique put forward the idea of a revolutionary praxis wherein art would be called upon to play the role of liberator. As for Debord, he inquired into the possibility of a "radical critique, with action, of daily life," that could mobilize, in the here and now, the mass of alienated individuals whom Lefebvre referred to.[45] He called for cultural revolution as the means to transform society and make daily life the theatre of ongoing, theatrical experimentation.

Defined first as "provocation" in *Liberté*, jazz became "insurrectional" and "an everyday revolutionary praxis" in the pages of *Parti pris*. In Straram's words, the jazzmen of the American East Coast were producing "ethics and aesthetics in tune with the political objectives of a total disalienation of man" by calling for their right to free, collective speech. For him, the "total man" was the one who opposed the entertainment industry, rebelled against white capitalist America, and tried to explode the dialectic entity of work, leisure, and private life. Free jazz especially contained enormous potential for mobilization because of its experimental dimension, its oppositional role, and its proximity to the social movements that were challenging American society during the 1960s. Which was why Straram wanted to publicize the music and situate it at the heart of daily life in Quebec. He pointed to the efforts that Groulx, Lefebvre, and Borremans were making to promote "jazz awareness, jazz practice, and jazz solidarity, right here."[46]

It was not just in Quebec that free jazz was seen as the soundtrack of the world revolution against capitalism and imperialism. Youth in France felt attracted by the music's ability to bring people together, and by the way musicians could put forward a collective identity without stifling individual voices. Vichy France (and its collaboration with the Nazis) was large in the national memory. Young people had had enough of ten years of Gaullist power and the legacy of a colonial empire only just dismantled at the end of the 1960s. The anti-authoritarian left was flexing its muscles to the rhythm of the student and worker demonstrations that led to the spontaneous uprising of May 68. In the midst of this atmosphere, Murray, Howard, Alan Shorter, Alan Silva, Marion Brown, and the Art Ensemble of Chicago stepped out of the plane in Paris. They discovered receptive audiences; their music presented itself as the sound equivalent of what was happening in the streets. After the events of May 68, free jazz maintained its status as subversive music thanks to, among others, the prominent *Jazz Magazine* writer Jean-Louis Comolli. French musical experimenters like François Tusques and Beb Guérin also helped stir the pot. These two men played with Murray, Silva, and Shorter and recorded *Intercommunal Music* with them in 1971. The disc is a record of the support offered by internationalist-minded French musicians to anti-imperialist struggles. Yet these musicians remained in the symbolic sphere of action only, due to the distance that separated them from African American players. Some journalists, in fact, accused them of illegitimately appropriating free jazz. Jazz Libre would have faced the same criticism if it weren't for the fact that the group's music aligned with the discourse around decolonization that was spread by the left-wing independence movement in Quebec.

By calling for a "necessary appropriation" of jazz, Straram was backing the idea that the condition of the proletariat in Quebec was analogous to that of the African diaspora in the United States.[47] First sketched out in *Revue socialiste* and *Parti pris*, the idea was taken up again by FLQ member Pierre Vallières in *White Niggers of America*:

> These niggers—who do not all have the same colour skin, who do not all speak the same language, who believe in different prophets, live in ghetto that are foreign to each other and experience in different ways the dictatorship of the same economic, political, and social system—all these niggers whom the partisans of slavery, the businessmen, and the politicians have for centuries contrived to set against each other (the better to exploit them and keep them powerless), know today that in this world of money, violence, and oppression, freedom and peace can be won only by the strength of numbers and of arms.[48]

Straram added his voice to the chorus by claiming:

> The cultural relationship obvious to me [...] is to be found in crucially accentuated form, and inexorably placed in its situation by the same necessity, that of insurrection in order to identify—and by a political option and deepening (in its many forms and also in the sense of societizing) the varieties of language.[49]

Starting out from this ideological postulate, Straram maintained that "only ignorance" could explain why the Quebec nation was not more aware of what bound it to the African diaspora in the United States.[50] According to him, jazz would fix this situation.

It is an obvious paradox that this metaphor was declaimed so intensely within the ranks of the leftist independence movement, even as its participants knew nothing, or virtually nothing, about Montreal's Black communities. Rather than seek to establish ties with them, Vallières and his accomplice of the time, Charles Gagnon, travelled to New York in 1966 with an eye to networking with African American activists, including members of the Black Panther Party. The experiences that Vallières had there and the books he read (most notably, those of Frantz Fanon, Albert Memmi, and Aimé Césaire) helped him grasp the strategies used to keep colonized peoples down and maintain white privilege. He saw a striking relationship between the subjugation of African Americans and the inferior position of "French Canadians" in the echelons of power governed by the English. For him, *négritude* was a condition, an attitude of resistance and affirmation, when faced with the political and economic hegemony of an oppressor. The idea of a white *négritude* put forward a racialized identity that referred to the double oppression (as a social class and as a nation) suffered by Quebeckers, according to the *Parti pris* way of seeing things.

Vallières's book attempted to legitimize this discourse and position the left-wing independence movement within the international optic of decolonization. But to reach his goal, he had to turn a blind eye to French Canada's slave-owning past and the demands of the various diasporas living in Montreal. He also had to convince his readership that Quebec's recent history was not stained by the spectre of racism, hence the supposed absence of an activist mindset among the Black community in Montreal.[51] David Austin would state that, when it comes down to it, the book participates in "a larger Canadian racial consciousness in which Blacks are both present and absent."[52] Straram, meanwhile, was a patron of the Little Burgundy nightclubs, though the musicians he mentioned to back up his arguments generally were only passing through. His silence about the jazzmen of the Harlem of the North matched that of the other *Parti pris* writers. Free jazz could exist in Quebec only through the revolt of politically alert white musicians, or so he seemed to be saying.

## Among the Spaniards

Straram and his *Parti pris* buddies were regulars at the Association Espagnole, and that was exactly where Jazz Libre showed up in the early winter of 1968, after they had been removed from the Jazz Workshop program. Not far from The Barrel, the triplex on Sherbrooke Street was a hot spot for the curious and the vinous, and included lefty intellectuals, FLQ sympathizers, politically minded artists, hard-core nationalists, and militants of all stripes. The alcohol flowed freely, discussions soon turned to screaming matches, but from them a strong fraternity emerged—men were in the majority in the place—along with the mixing and matching of ideas needed to create an eventual consensus over the Quebec question. Jazz Libre joined the fun by moving their instruments up to the third floor of this refuge that, according to legend, Pedro Rubio-Dumont founded for expatriate anarchists and communists who could not tolerate the atmosphere of Franco's Spain.

The members of Jazz Libre found both an audience and a community at the Association Espagnole. The friendships they made there pushed them—especially the horn players—further to the left. Charbonneau was receptive to the *Parti pris* ideas because of his working-class background. The eldest of the group felt very much at home, since he had had experience with artistic circles where revolt was the order of the day. That was just at the time when *White Niggers of America* rolled off the presses. As well as the *Parti pris* gang, the members of the group rubbed shoulders with Groulx and Borremans, poets Gaston Miron and Gilbert Langevin, painter Serge Lemoyne, sculptor Armand Vaillancourt, and singer Pauline Julien. The place was the official nerve centre of the underground, the "semi-clandestine crossroads for the builders of the nationalist explosion."[53] In Straram's words, this was where "inventiveness in art could give birth to Quebec society from its own deliverance."[54] Starting on January 26, 1968, on Thursday and Sunday evenings, Jazz Libre provided the soundtrack for that beery march toward Quebec's future. Enthusiastic at what he was hearing, Pierre Boisvert summed up the arrival of Jazz Libre at the Association Espagnole: "In the hands of the white niggers of America, free jazz, the symbol of Black Power, took root in Quebec."[55]

***

The appropriation of free jazz might seem surprising, considering the difficulties jazz musicians had making a living in Montreal at the end of the 1960s. This period may well have been "the end of an era," but Thouin and the others in the band saw things in a different light.[56] Jazz Libre avoided the fate of other groups simply because it inhabited the margins of the scene. On one hand, the quartet soldiered on despite being pushed out of The Barrel's Jazz Workshop. On the other, its music left the players no other option than to distance themselves from a milieu that had little use for their music. Later, Thouin would state that the group's journey marked a break in the story of jazz in the city.[57] If it is true that, musically, he and his bandmates broke with the preceding generation, they did find an audience and attract the interest of critics thanks to the pioneering work of earlier artists who had pushed jazz forward and called attention to it. Building from there, Jazz Libre followed the path of socially engaged music on the left and fulfilled the expectations of artists and intellectuals who had been preparing the way for free jazz in the province through the 1960s. Cocke could not suspect, when he celebrated the arrival of a "made-in-Quebec jazz bomb," that Préfontaine and his brothers were intending to go beyond the simple search for new forms of music.[58]

[2]

# A Detour via Rock Music (1968–1970)

*And then there were the Jazz Libre musicians, a bunch of wild individualists whose syncopated savage sounds and sobs would blow your ears off your head and could be listened to only by a select few who would drop in on them from time to time. [...] What they brought to Charlebois was something no other singer had, and that very few artists anywhere in the world enjoyed: a back-up group that kept striving to do more and better [...], who were not content to just "accompany," but who were an important part of the show themselves.*[1]

–Yves Leclerc

JAZZ LIBRE HAD BEEN improvising at the Association Espagnole for only a couple of weeks when they decided to experiment with abstract projections. From February 8 to 25, 1968, the quartet worked with Lucie Barash, the co-founder of a collective that had perfected the use of slides and liquid light to put on psychedelic shows. But Barash's images were not to Jean Préfontaine's liking; he thought the visual component distracted audiences who were not particularly well versed in free jazz. "The psychedelic style scatters attention, it's a bombardment of multiple sensations. In the case of our music, people need to be able to concentrate," he told Emmanuel Cocke in an interview.[2] Still, Jazz Libre remained optimistic about finding a visual equivalent to their music action. The search was on, since the group did want to meet other artists whose work was based on experiments with form and language.

The Association Espagnole was without a doubt the place for such encounters. And that was where Jazz Libre crossed paths with Robert Charlebois, the rock singer with whom they would share the stage for a little more than a year, from spring 1968 to the end of summer 1969. The group was drawn into the singer's world of rock happenings. Jazz Libre discovered what fame was and dove into psychedelic culture, despite Préfontaine's reservations. The fall of 1969 saw the group move further into the counterculture movement that had taken off in Quebec after Expo 67. They began to play with L'Infonie, a singular pluridisciplinary band that could number up to twenty members, and in the process, Jazz Libre moved closer to that part of largely apolitical Quebec youth in search of new experiences. Though it was a prolific time, this interlude did slow the quartet's efforts to define their music and invest it with a social purpose. As I will explain in this chapter, most of all, it catalyzed a schism in the group as it tried to negotiate the borders between showbiz and counterculture.

## The High Priests of Free Rock

The meeting between Jazz Libre and Robert Charlebois was a determining moment for both parties. The singer already had three albums to his name. The first two reflected the path he had taken since he first appeared on stage at the Butte-à-Mathieu, warming up for Félix Leclerc. At that point, he was working in a folk style. The third album bore the mark of American counterculture in which Charlebois had immersed himself starting in 1967. He spent three months in Los Angeles, in the heart of the hippie world, and heard the emblematic bands of the time, such as Fraternity of Man and Big Brother and the Holding Company. He tried to cozy up to musicians he met during substance-filled evenings but came to realize that his music was out of touch with what was being done in California and that he would do well to work with other creators instead of just on his own. "That's when I started wanting to work with free jazz musicians. I understood that was the basis of good art: to surround yourself with top players."[3]

The counterculture epicentre, California was the place where young people were expressing their revolt and pursuing their utopias. Back in those days, they dreamed of transforming the United States from its imperialist, reactionary, and dehumanizing condition, with its cult of technocracy and alienating social norms, into something new. The hippie revolution, though polymorphous, took on three forms: sexual, psychedelic, and musical—rock music. The third was what got Charlebois's attention.

Changed by his West Coast journey, the singer decided to undertake a "massive freeing-up operation" to escape the dead end of Quebec folk (the *chansonniers* tradition) and Quebec pop (the Beatles-inspired *yéyé*) that strictly adhered to the particular codes of those genres.[4] Singers like Claude Gauthier, Jean-Pierre Ferland, and Gilles Vigneault, to name a few, with their acoustic instrumentation and French poetic lyrics, struggled to keep up with the rhythmic dance beats of the *yéyé* bands of the time (among them, Caesar and the Romans, the Baronets, and the Hou-Lops) that took their inspiration from British and American rock. Charlebois belonged to the *chansonniers* current when he left for Los Angeles. What he heard there moved him to break down the borders separating folk singers from pop bands and create something original that would speak to the Quebec nation's place in North America (its *américanité*) and its distinctiveness in the French-speaking world (its *québécité*). The daring rock styles of California artists like Frank Zappa and the Mothers of Invention, The Grateful Dead, and Jefferson Airplane were laying down new ways of self-expression through improvisation and experimentation. Contemplating the stage and sound excesses of rock, Charlebois saw a way to free himself from the paralyzing conventions he had learned and that—to his eyes and ears—characterized the performing arts in Quebec.

Charlebois had studied theatre and understood that a musical revue could be a good vehicle for his own personal rock revolution. He had a good amount of experience with this kind of performance thanks to his participation in shows like *Yéyé versus chansonniers* and *Terre des bums*. With comedian and performer Yvon Deschamps and two old friends from the National Theatre School, Claudine Monfette (alias Mouffe) and Louise Forestier, he began designing an event, part provocation and part collective awakening, that would stir audiences and performers alike. The show would have to be put together quickly, since the troupe had a window that had suddenly opened in the programming of the Théâtre de Quat'sous in Montreal. Paul Buissonneau, its co-founder, supported Charlebois and his group at first, but he backed off when he discovered the degree of anarchy that reigned on stage. "Arrangez-vous avec votre hostie d'show!" ("Figure out your damned show yourself!") he reputedly shouted at Charlebois—and so the name of the performance was born.[5] The organizational disorder, and not the half-improvised fusion of rock with sketches and monologues, had Buissonneau worried. Writer Bruno Roy would call the result "liberating disorder" in his study of what came to be known as the *Osstidcho*.[6]

The musical revue was in its infancy when Charlebois heard Jazz Libre for the first time. The group was beginning its second stand at the Association Espagnole and showed no signs of fatigue as far as musical deconstruction was concerned. Having learned in California that he needed to be surrounded by top players, Charlebois invited Jean Préfontaine, Yves Charbonneau, Guy Thouin, and Maurice Richard to join him on stage. Though it sounded unlikely at first, the idea of accompanying a rock singer slowly filtered into the group's collective mind, partly thanks to Thouin, who convinced his confreres to take a chance. The four jazzmen saw an opportunity to expand the audience for their music (there were rarely more than twenty people listening to them at the Association Espagnole) while testing their ability to interact with new creative partners. Once the deal was inked, Charlebois hurried to incorporate the quartet into the team. "I found the best musicians in the world!" he enthused to Forestier.[7] She was less eager to share the stage with "those big beer-drinkers from the Association Espagnole."[8] But she accepted Charlebois's casting, knowing she could count on pianist Jacques Perron to supply the show's rhythmic and harmonic structure.

Though they came from different horizons, Jazz Libre, Charlebois, and Forestier seemed to share a number of political preoccupations. They had all participated in *Poèmes et chansons de la résistance* ("poems and songs from the resistance"), a show that played on May 28, 1968, the evening before the premier of *Osstidcho*. The Comité d'Aide au Groupe Vallières-Gagnon and singer Pauline Julien coordinated the event that raised money for the defence of FLQ members Pierre Vallières and Charles Gagnon, at the same time promoting their designation as "political prisoners," which would hopefully ensure better conditions for the revolutionary leftist nationalists imprisoned in Canadian jails. The two FLQ members were arrested when they returned from the United States the previous year and were accused of murder and setting off bombs, part of their involvement in terrorist actions that had led to the accidental death of Thérèse Morin on May 5, 1966. She was the secretary of the boss of a shoe factory that had been on strike for several months.

That show (*Poèmes et chansons de la résistance*) attested to the increasing politicization of the performing arts scene in Quebec, even if very few artists adhered to the FLQ's revolutionary discourse and spontaneous practices. Jazz Libre and its new fellow musicians showed up at the Gesù hall accompanied by a couple dozen artists who had agreed to play for free in "an evening of solidarity."[9] Among them: pianist François Dansereau, poets Gilbert Langevin and Claude Gauvreau, singers Raymond Lévesque, Georges Dor, and Tex Lecor, as well as actresses Ginette Letondal, Hélène Loiselle, and Michèle Rossignol. Journalist Claude Gingras, in an article that came out the next day, pointed out that Jazz Libre was creating "a form of expression closest to today's reality," while Charlebois and Forestier "showed that they are truly on the front lines of artistic expression."[10] The show was a success and played across Quebec, in Hull, Trois-Rivières, Sherbrooke, and Quebec City, in October of that same year. The projects of the leftist independence movement definitely found resonance in the popular culture of the time.

Jazz Libre stepped on stage at the Théâtre de Quat'sous for the premiere of *Osstidcho* less than twenty-four hours after their performance at the Gesù. It was 8:30 in the evening on Pine Avenue, just east of Saint Lawrence Boulevard, and all 150 seats in the little theatre were taken. Gingras commented:

> No curtain. The stage is occupied by a giant metal scaffolding. You're in the mood even before the show begins. Soon, one by one, the performers come on stage and begin to climb the scaffold. [...] The guys from Jazz Libre have some trouble doing that, since they are wearing long, colourful robes, like high priests who are going to officiate from above. The other performers, in chalk-white costumes, follow them, only to climb back down to earth.[11]

The first part of the show began in impromptu fashion with a suite of tunes sung by Forestier and Charlebois. The "total musical madness" took its time arriving, Gingras remarked with some disenchantment. The second part—a long number, some forty minutes, with the two singers plus Mouffe and Deschamps—was closer to the image of the happening that everyone was waiting for. The performers worked around monologues spontaneously revamped by Deschamps to the rhythm of various songs and sketches. In the background, "the harsh but authentic cries of free jazz—really, very free."[12] The troupe served up another helping the next evening with greater spontaneity and originality. The result: the dozens of shows at the Théâtre de Quat'sous were followed by a further week at the Comédie Canadienne in September (called *Osstidcho king size*), then extra dates were added at the very imposing Wilfrid-Pelletier Hall at the Place des Arts in January of the next year (called, this time, *Osstidcho meurt*—"the show dies").

Jazz Libre attempted to find its place during this nine-month adventure. The group accompanied Forestier and Charlebois when they sang numbers from their repertory. The rhythm section remained faithful to the scores, while the horns took off on dissonant forays. The quartet was also given ten minutes or so during intermission to lay down its free jazz as it wished. Unstoppable, or almost, the band tried to add extra minutes to the time allowed. At the Comédie Canadienne, the four musicians asserted themselves even more and raised the level of their intensity. Gingras called it "verbal and sound delirium when, for instance, the singers' words [...] are drowned out by the noise of the instruments and the audience protests, some because of the infernal noise, and others because they can't understand the words."[13] The on-stage dynamics were hardly better at the Place des Arts, since there was no scaffolding to contain Jazz Libre. The new configuration put the horns front and centre, much to the dismay of Forestier. "Anarchy is great at the tavern, but anarchy on stage [...] has to be staged, it has to be organized. [...] You can't go against the laws of acoustics. You can't come and screech in my right ear while I'm improvising on Robert's harmonies."[14] The tension between Forestier and Jazz Libre might not have been obvious to the audience, but it certainly spoiled the vibe that the first version of *Osstidcho* was based on.

The quartet's new self-assertiveness was due in part to the confidence it picked up after a recording session, on December 4 and 5, 1968, that resulted in an album co-produced by London Records of Canada and Radio-Canada International. Jazz Libre got that opportunity after *Osstidcho king size* and the autumn tour of *Poèmes et chansons de la résistance*. The group wanted to let people hear what it had been up to since the summer of 1967. The album's liner notes by Edward Farrant explained it this way:

> There is no rhythm, or more accurately, no easily discernible rhythm, no time or key signatures, no formal structure in the compositions, no imposed harmonies or chord progressions, and more often than not no theme or melody. Freed from these traditional elements which hinder direct expression, each member can transmit his emotions directly to his instrument: the saxophone laments or revolts, the trumpet cries or calls to arms, the bass escapes into another world of electronic sounds, and the drum shatters a military march rhythm after only a few bars to express disapproval of the military, the Vietnam war, or Biafra. At times a definite key signature will

> impose itself, or other traditional elements will be used momentarily out of sarcasm or derision: snatches of a sugary "pop" song, a banal rhythm, a waltz or military march. On the other hand there is an attempt to discover new sounds, new possibilities of each instrument. Many of these sounds are not notes, not even "normal" sounds, but "noises."[15]

All the same, Thouin sometimes tried to insert signposts here and there so that Jazz Libre would not stumble in-to absolute "musical nihilism."[16] He recruited pianist Pierre Nadeau and gave him the responsibility of adding harmonic and rhythmic support to the group during its more audacious wanderings. Thouin had in mind pianist Cecil Taylor's music; his album *Unit Structures*, from 1966, was necessary listening for anyone interested in free jazz. With the agreement of all, Jazz Libre became a quintet as it recorded works like "Opus 2," "Valse à grand'mère," and "Il n'avait jamais fait si beau si longtemps."

Préfontaine and his colleagues began the year 1969 with a sense of self-assurance, though their busy schedules left them little time to venture into new musical explorations. They spent most of January and February on the road with the *Osstidcho meurt* crew, then accompanied Charlebois and Forestier during the second half of March. The duo had just finished recording material for an album. Jazz Libre was part of those sessions, and they earned international recognition after their 45 rpm record, which included "California" and "Lindberg," came out in France. Everyone put their money on the first side, but in the end, "Lindberg," the B side, won the day with its Quebec dialect, colourful (for France) swear words, and jazzy psychedelic tune.

Intrigued, an agency called Europe 1 invited the Charlebois–Forestier duo and the Jazz Libre musicians to play in Paris—a series of concerts at the Olympia where they were to share the program with singer Georgette Plana, originally a music hall performer, and Antoine, a sort of Donovan clone. Forestier called him "the latest hippy star [...] who supposedly plays rock."[17] The tour would crown the work done over the past year. Charlebois, Forestier, and Jazz Libre hit Paris, ready to take on the Olympia, where, the previous year, Frank Zappa had won over French audiences. The Quebeckers would have a two-week stay beginning March 26, 1969, with twenty minutes every evening to convince their Old Europe cousins that Quebec rock meant something.

The battle was far from won. From the very first evening, Charlebois and his gang came up against an audience with little sympathy for their on-stage excesses:

> The two are a disturbing presence. He screams. She hoots. He tremolos. She hollers. A demented, convulsive soundscape surrounds them. With her poncho and headband, she looks like a miniature squaw. And he, an operatic trapper with the electric hairdo of an angry hedgehog. [...] Every night, the two Canadians splash through a sea of incomprehension.[18]

The band had problems with the sound, and the Olympia's technicians were uncooperative. The group's inebriated condition and their bellicose, even insolent, attitude did not help their cause.

Unlike the others, Forestier was not intoxicated. Hostility grew between her and the rest of the group. She had to share the spotlight with Charlebois, who had just won the Prix Félix Leclerc at the Festival du Disque Canadien back in Montreal. In Paris, Forestier sang "not with Robert, but next to Robert."[19] Even worse, she had to negotiate with Préfontaine and Charbonneau, who were determined to occupy centre stage. The two horns went on blowing in her ears and perverting the arrangements, while Charlebois seemed ever less concerned with winning over the French. Bruno Coquatrix, the director general of the Olympia, finally lost patience with the "delinquents."[20] On Sunday, April 6, he brought down the curtain on the Quebeckers after Thouin, exasperated by the excesses of his stage partners, abandoned his post and Charlebois, suddenly overcome with the desire to play a drum solo, accidentally sent a snare drum heading toward the audience.

The band's gig at the Olympia ended a week sooner than scheduled. "The Charlebois scandal" was front-page news back in Quebec and did wonders for the singer's career. "The savage from Canada ruffled French feathers" and "Quebec's Jazz Libre swept off the Olympia stage," announced the headline in *La Patrie*.[21] Like several other newspapers, *La Presse* reported that "Charlebois was shown the door at the Olympia" after having thrown parts of one of the two drum kits used by the group.[22] The adventure on French soil was recorded by filmmakers François Brault and Jean Dansereau in *À soir on fait peur au monde* ("tonight we scare people") in 1969. A true "poem to Charlebois," this rockumentary gave Forestier and Jazz Libre secondary roles while taking care not to demystify the group's misadventures at the Olympia.[23]

The beginning of 1969 was Jazz Libre's initiation into showbiz. It began when impresario Guy Latraverse took over the production of *Osstidcho king size* and became both Deschamps's and Charlebois's agent. "Like a cultural happening, *Osstidcho* expanded the borders of what a show could be. Nothing—and we all knew it—would be the way it was before," Latraverse later said.[24] For Forestier, that change meant she would have to sing three feet from her stage partner. "At the Comédie Canadienne, it was tolerable. [...] But at the Place des Arts, show business took over everything once and for all."[25] As for Mouffe, she would call this tumultuous adventure "a human disaster."[26]

Jazz Libre also seemed to fade during this sojourn on the frontiers of showbiz. The group was renamed Rock Libre du Québec when *À soir on fait peur au monde* hit the movie theatres in October 1969—at least that was what the film's credits and the 45 rpm record that came out at the same time suggested. The origins of the new name are obscure. "Rock Libre du Québec" facilitated the inclusion of musicians like Perron, Michel Robidoux, and Pierre Ringuette, who at times accompanied Charlebois and Forestier, without their necessarily being part of Jazz Libre. The name hinted at the group's move toward rock at the expense of free jazz, and also pointed to the need to break with the entity that had existed on its own, alongside the singer. By substituting Rock Libre for Jazz Libre (or free rock for free jazz), Charlebois would not have to share the glory with artists whom Latraverse essentially considered backup players. From full-fledged partners, Thouin and his colleagues were slowly but surely relegated to the status "of ordinary employees" paid according to the rate established by the musicians' union.[27] Disillusionment and bitterness settled over the quartet during the winter of 1969, but the group's monetary needs and their desire to reach wider audiences had them deciding to go back and work with Charlebois, even after the fiasco at the Olympia. They were part of the lineup at the Esquire and warmed up for Steppenwolf at the Toronto Pop Festival and the Montreal Forum at the end of June.

This chapter lasted a little over a year, since everyone benefited from it. Charlebois told journalist Denise Boucher, shortly after *Osstidcho king size*, that he pictured a prolific future for the four jazzmen: "With them, I'm going to work hard. If I can manage to live with those musicians, I'm sure we could have a big party that will last five years. l like those guys."[28] The separation between Jazz Libre and Charlebois was the perfect occasion to evaluate what the quartet brought to the singer's career. Journalist Yves Leclerc wrote that the collaboration helped the singer stand out from the rest of Quebec's soundscape at the end of the 1960s. Leclerc praised those "talented wildmen who categorically refused to be dominated or beaten down by Charlebois's strong personality."[29] The man in question was in absolute agreement. "Their challenge, the fact that the guys challenged me, made that album [recorded with Forestier in 1968] into something that can't be classified and will never go out of style."[30] But he did add, and with reason, "Still, I did manage to get Jazz Libre to play the same chords together."[31] He was clearly helped out by Thouin, "who could beat his kit like a rock drummer," Richard, "who was attracted both by free jazz and hard rock," and Robidoux, who played the crucial role of "musical reconciler" on the guitar.[32]

In the end, Jazz Libre's work with Charlebois was much more than a simple change in musical landscape. It redrew the lines between *américanité* and *québécité* in the cultural sphere. Jazz Libre and Charlebois were following similar paths in 1968 and 1969. They urged their audiences to picture a new image of themselves as a French-speaking people in North America. *Osstidcho* depended on spontaneity and the mixing of languages to stage—and then concretize—the movement of a French Canadian to a Québécois identity. This "demonstrative act" worked more in the cultural than the political sphere. Yet it did add to the growing talk about national self-determination.[33] Jean-Pierre Sirois-Trahan would state that *Osstidcho* "was the place where a collective voice was heard from which a Quebec future might emerge."[34] But the shape of this future remained too vague for Jazz Libre, especially since the pressures exercised by the showbiz industry disturbed the group's cohesion.

## The Infoniaques

Jazz Libre wandered in the wilderness during their fifteen months with Charlebois, but that did not stop the group from trying to establish durable ties with other artists who shared their political and artistic preoccupations. The quartet could count on poet and jazzophile Raôul

Duguay. Born in Val-d'Or, a mining town in northern Quebec, Duguay moved to Montreal at the beginning of the 1960s to undertake doctoral studies in philosophy. He had an interest in phonetics and the musicality of the French language as well as in being a trumpet player. He participated in the founding of *Passe-Partout*, a literary journal, and, in 1966, published a first collection where jazz and poetry shook hands. With titles like "swing de l'instinct" ("the instinct swing"), "enjazzement des sangs" ("jazz in the blood"), and "be-bop des eaux intérieures" ("be-bop of the sea within"), *Ruts* declared its fealty to jazz. The book illustrated Patrick Straram's insistence that "jazz is a determining factor in daily life" for poets in Quebec.[35] During the same period, Duguay improvised to Miles Davis's music as part of a poetry recital, laying down the foundation for his work that would take him to Expo 67, where he met Walter Boudreau and his musicians.

Jazz occupied an enviable spot at the Youth Pavilion at Expo 67. Cocke was running the cultural programming, combining visual arts, jazz, and poetry. Duguay and Boudreau met during these "Jazzpo" sessions at the beginning of the summer. On October 26, as the centennial festivities were winding down, Duguay and Boudreau's trio took to the stage to present "L'amour suprême," a poem inspired by the four-part suite recorded by John Coltrane and his quartet three years earlier, the famous *A Love Supreme*. The poet's new work was dedicated to the genius saxman, but also to Che Guevara, Vietnam's National Liberation Front, and to "the people working for Quebec liberation."[36]

Duguay had been contributing to *Parti pris* for a year when he performed his "L'amour suprême" at Expo 67.

Being involved with the journal had him listening to jazz in a more radical way. He met up with Paul Chamberland, a former colleague from the Université de Montréal, as well as rubbed shoulders with Straram. He was the literary critic at *Parti pris*, so he did not write about music in its pages, but he did describe his way of seeing things in *Quoi*, a magazine he co-founded at the beginning of 1967.

> The cry of QUÉBEC is like that of *négritude* […], and that is the connection to jazz. my cry before an audience is jazzistic in word and in deed. it is the trance of my being. it carries a decantation of folk rhythms. jig. rigadoon. out of nostalgia for the future of the race. like jazz at its origins. my poem is a song of revolt. a slave's lament. the cry issuing from the very heart of the quebec alienated individual. cry that. will finally rise in a saving grace [sic].[37]

Thérèse Dumouchel, who wrote a column in *Parti pris* called "Les arts zartistiques," lost no time echoing her colleague. She quoted him at length and concluded, "Exorcism of our *négritude* from the first line to the last, DUGUAY's poetry is overdetermined against the back-ground of our collective unconscious."[38] *Parti pris* also published "d'amour suprême à," a poem along the lines of "L'amour suprême," backing up Straram's ideas about jazz and Duguay's use of it.[39]

Préfontaine, Thouin, Charbonneau, and Richard were on familiar ground when they accepted Duguay's offer to join the "Total Poem" that was to be read on May 1, 1968, at the Bibliothèque Nationale, then situated at 1700 St-Denis

Street in Montreal. The event would kick off Poetry Week, involving just about all the players in literary Montreal. Poets, publishers, and booksellers took part in this event piloted by the Direction des Manifestations Culturelles, a provincial cultural events office created six months earlier. Entitled *Abébécaire Babel II*, Duguay's show was an astonishing patchwork of art forms (music, poetry, film, sculpture, and painting) designed to dazzle the audience. "I will perform collective therapy [...] by forcing people to participate and react, which is not what they're used to doing," he explained.[40] Positioned at opposite ends of the hall, Jazz Libre and Boudreau's group provided the improvised soundtrack for this "total art show" designed as a manifesto against the Vietnam War.[41]

The project was of its time. It took the experiments undertaken by other groups and tried to make them accessible to a wider audience. The idea was to break down the barriers between art forms and rethink the limits of what a show could be. Already, back in 1965, the members of Zirmate (Jean Sauvageau, Rona Nereida, Serge Lemoyne, Gilles Chartier, Claude Péloquin, and several others) were offering avant-garde theatrical performances, bringing together popular culture, poetry, electronic music, film projections, and in situ painting in hopes of "throwing the audience for a loop and shaking up commonly held ideas and psychic realities to create revelations of all kinds."[42] A true precursor through its Dada-inspired happenings, Zirmate offered a brand of liberating, non-bourgeois culture. Chamberland wrote in *Parti pris* that the troupe underlined the key issue, which was the artist's role as a person who creates awareness in society.[43] Zirmate's interdisciplinary improvisations did not aim for a mass audience, but they did show the way for other intrepid creators. Among them were Charlebois and his accomplices in *Osstidcho* and Duguay, who also knew how to surround himself with the right people.

Duguay valued Jazz Libre's approach and the way they were trying to create active listening among the audience. On Radio-Canada, he explained that the group "might disconcert people who can't make the effort of the mind or open themselves totally to emotion." He added, "To those who don't hear anything, we could say, 'It's not what you hear in this music that disturbs your mind and your ear, it's what you don't hear.'"[44] As did Straram, Duguay and Jazz Libre gave priority to politically engaged, active listening, but their paths crossed only intermittently in the year that followed the performance of *Abébécaire Babel II*, since the quartet was busy with its *Osstidcho* partners.

All that changed in autumn of 1969. The break with Charlebois left Jazz Libre free to get together with Duguay and Boudreau again. The latter had recently stepped away from jazz to move into the study of contemporary music. In 1968, he wrote "Apocalypse" and used a May 23 concert in the city of Sorel, downriver from Montreal, to recruit the core of musicians with whom he would establish the group L'Infonie. Jazz Libre was part of that concert, and Thouin used the ties between his group and Boudreau's to launch the idea of a pluridisciplinary band with membership that could vary and could play in different ways depending on the context. Jazz Libre joined L'Infonie from its stage debut in the fall of 1969. The name "Infonie," an inversion of *symphonie* (at first the group's name was spelled

"Inphonie"), pointed to the group's desire to rethink the paradigms of orchestral music and its relation to society. This unusual and whimsical orchestra consisted of up to twenty members: trumpeters, sax players, guitarists, bass players, percussionists, pianists, and trombonists, as well as painters, poets, and a "storyteller."[45] Among these people was saxman Gaby Johnston, "a little bit of a revolutionary," who did a stint with Préfontaine in Jazz Libre for a few months in early 1970.[46]

The "Infoniaques," under Boudreau's direction and urged on by Duguay's verbal delirium, "wanted to go further than Robert Charlebois" when it came to remaking Quebec's musical creativity.[47] "Since total sound totality exists in the Mind and that everything sings everywhere allthetime in the Great Micro-Macro ALLNESS, L'Infonie is just the humble spout of Breath reflecting and polysonorous of Light," thus spoke Duguay in the manifesto he crafted for the group.[48] Boudreau put it in more concise terms: "We are in the simplest of ways a group of researchers."[49] Which was why L'Infonie assembled a multitude of idioms (from jazz to rock with a stop-off at the rigadoon and contemporary music) while engaging in both collective improvisation and written music.

The name "Infonie" echoed the inner revolution the group was aiming for in the spirit of the times. Through a semantic shift of "inner" borrowed from English, the negative prefix "in" came to signify the sounds and voices that issued from the deepest depths of the band's members. "L'Infonie does some pretty hip things. L'Infonie builds up the outside through an inner voice," Claude St-Germain sermonized.[50] Duguay added, "If Everyone Began by Realizing in their

Own Person the Itinerant work of Art, Everyone Would Be Environed with Autonomy and Originality."[51] L'Infonie was right in step with the counterculture movements that were up and running in Quebec. With the inner revolution taking precedence over political action, art became a tool for transforming individual minds, considered as the only vectors capable of creating true social change.

This new attitude toward confronting power was largely a reaction to the events that shook the United States at the end of the 1960s. The year 1968 was particularly hard for the young generation dreaming of changing their society through political action like the civil rights campaign, the new student left, and the anti-war movement. In April, Martin Luther King Jr. was assassinated. Two months later, Democratic candidate Robert F. Kennedy fell victim to the same fate. Rudi Dutschke, a European student movement leader and inspiration for the American New Left, was also targeted by an assassin.[52] In August, the Chicago Police Department, charged with protecting the Democratic Party convention in that city, ran amok in what was later called a police riot; their repression was aimed at youth protesting the Vietnam War. Republican Richard Nixon won the presidency several months later, leaving militants wondering about their tactics. To stave off disillusionment, and perhaps out of self-protection, counterculture youth began to believe that societal change would come about only through personal growth and increased consciousness. Yoga, health foods, going back to the land, and simplicity all became personal forms of the revolution that would turn individuals into forces for change. Though less challenged by their society, young people in Quebec were also drawn to the idea of a peaceful, universalist utopia.

As in the United States, Quebec counterculture was hard to pin down, multifaceted, and polymorphous. It, too, declared itself apolitical insofar as its opposition to power took place "outside of areas where power relations normally express themselves."[53] It wanted to step away from the paradigms of left-wing nationalism in its search for an "alternative Quebec."[54] Society would be transformed through new ways of seeing individuals and their relation to the world—and the cosmos too—instead of through shared struggles the way leftist groups operated. Experiments of all types (new moral codes, but also spirituality and communal experiences) were what the youth counterculture had in mind as it yearned to escape the power of the state, the Church, and the family. Music, either played or listened to, was an integral part of this inner revolution. And L'Infonie saw itself at the forefront.

Jazz Libre was particularly prolific during the few months they spent with the group. Préfontaine and his bandmates were part of the first two recordings L'Infonie made (Richard missed the second session, however). Engineered and produced by André Perry, the first is a heterogeneous mash-up of free jazz, psychedelic rock, and classical music, including an orchestrated interpretation of the Beatles' "She's Leaving Home" followed by Johann Sebastian Bach's "Agnus Dei." In between those pieces were a number of free-form freak-outs and playful vocal interventions. Coproduced by L'Infonie and Tony Roman, the second record, *Mantra*, is a very credible revisiting of the piece "In C" by the American minimalist composer Terry Riley. Jazz Libre felt right at home with L'Infonie's repertory; the "free-jazz-new-now-thing-think" was part—along with "white-hot psychedelics under a mop of hair"—of the group's "musical possibilities."[55] The quartet had its share of playing time, since it generally took to the stage during the first part of each evening with L'Infonie, reaching the same audience it had gigged for with Charlebois.

The perfect fusion between Jazz Libre and L'Infonie was, however, impossible in the long term. First of all, the project was not financially viable. It cost a lot of money to move the collective around Quebec: $1,000 to get them to play outside of Montreal. Valois would remark with a wry smile that the honoraria received was often less than the bar bills accumulated by Charbonneau, Préfontaine, and Johnston. Either L'Infonie was not always paid what was owed by contract, or the three musicians downed an enormous amount of alcohol. A combination of the two is more likely.

Préfontaine and Charbonneau wanted to go back for good to total collective improvisation, both in form and in the decision-making process—in other words, to be without the "authoritarian structure of a conductor and musicians, which is a structure that makes free jazz impossible."[56] Thouin was stimulated by L'Infonie's internal dynamics, and Richard was willing to go along too, but the horns were less and less inclined to give in to Boudreau's musical direction. The break was less the fruit of a personality conflict and more the inevitable result of political and artistic differences. On both sides, it was a friendly au revoir.

Meanwhile, Duguay was trying to distance himself from the leftist revolution by making L'Infonie serve another brand that he hoped would be kinder:

If we have chosen art over politics, it's because

> art is a joint. Through art we recover the pleasure of creation, the chance to be human, and not malicious. Through art we will try and find the best position so the sun will shine on our faces. L'Infonie does not want to project the image of misery [...] on life, as it is done so often in Quebec. Everyone here, in their inner space, has to become a King.[57]

His position had him questioning the radical politics that, little by little, became Charbonneau and Préfontaine's main motivation. Still, L'Infonie remained a "commune in its founding idea," where the diversity of points of view and practices was accepted and even encouraged.[58] Diversity was no obstacle to Jazz Libre joining L'Infonie at first, but the quartet felt less and less at home in this "kind of hippie community."[59] In the spring of 1970, Préfontaine and Charbonneau decided to finally begin their search for revolutionary praxis after two years of wandering the grey zone between showbiz and counterculture.

***

In the end, Jazz Libre's time with L'Infonie exposed the latent tensions already present when the group played with Charlebois. Musically, Préfontaine and Charbonneau adopted an increasingly combative and inflexible stance during 1970. They rejected any kind of structure (rhythmic, harmonic, tonal, etc.) or writing that would have hampered totally free collective improvisation. The group's December 1968 album was the result of the players' efforts at conciliation, but the horns were in no mood to compromise at the beginning of the new decade. The two men wanted to return to their music action and give it a much more political orientation, along *Parti pris* lines. When they came back from Paris, they explained to journalist Jacques Larue-Langlois that their music would now begin to reflect their belief in socialism. Thouin settled for pointing out that he lived "in a capitalist country," while Richard proclaimed himself an anarchist, though without much conviction.[60] Then he added he was thinking of getting involved in other musical projects so as not to stagnate within the ranks of Jazz Libre. Richard would not leave the group, but he was often absent, starting in the autumn of 1969, forcing his bandmates to find replacements for him.

Meanwhile, Thouin was coming to see that his artistic concerns were incompatible with Jazz Libre's political orientation. He did not subscribe to the "musical nihilism" that seemed to attract Préfontaine and Charbonneau: "The musical experience of playing free has a certain duration. Then it has to become aesthetic, too."[61] Thouin turned to serious studies in classical percussion at McGill University when Jazz Libre and Charlebois decided to go in different directions. He was also interested in contemporary works: among others, the concrete music of French composer Pierre Boulez and the German serialism of Karlheinz Stockhausen. "The best way to get our form of music to evolve is to listen to other forms," he told Larue-Langlois.[62] Thouin's experience with L'Infonie fed his sense of exploration and moved him further from Jazz Libre's music action. The break was inevitable, especially once he announced his intention to travel to India and learn to play the tabla under a guru. He would not follow his long-time bandmates in the spring of 1970 when they split from L'Infonie and put their music in the service of the Quebec revolution.

[3]

# Countercultural Jazz Vibes (1968–1970)

*A Concert-Forum is a concert where everyone, audience and musicians alike, discusses music, liberation, creation, new ways of living and being, and the experiences we have with other people. The music that everyone knows, that surrounds us, either commercial music or the kind we are getting closer to now, the free jazz we have only just now heard.*[1]

–Pierre Cadieux

THE PERIOD FROM spring of 1968 to spring of 1970 saw Jazz Libre work with Robert Charlebois and L'Infonie. The quartet had its hours of glory during those two years, but it also put up with the vicissitudes of showbiz with a sense of bitterness and growing impatience. The feeling of wandering in the wilderness did not stop the group from promoting its music to younger audiences. It wanted to be closer to Quebec youth, and so it oriented its music action toward them after being relegated to the margins of the Montreal jazz scene. The counterculture revolt was at its peak at the end of the 1960s, and Jazz Libre saw the opportunity to prove free jazz's ability to mobilize in a context of political and cultural upheaval. Despite its busy schedule, the group set out to initiate Quebec's young people into its music, using concert forums staged on various campuses in Montreal and outside the city, starting in 1968. The quartet was simply following Patrick Straram's lead in his quest to propagandize for jazz.

This initiative ran alongside the projects started by the Technique d'Action Sociale unit, a subgroup of the Fusion des Arts collective, whose mandate was to bring together different art forms to democratize creative expression and raise the political awareness of its audiences. Jazz Libre rubbed elbows with these artists at the Association Espagnole; the quartet's idea of concert forums sprang from that encounter. The two groups did not travel alongside each other for very long, but they did produce a number of events, and the quartet, under this influence, went on to program activities designed for counterculture youth. Jazz Libre had little time to spare, being busy with Charlebois and L'Infonie, but those projects brought little satisfaction, since they could not turn music action into a true social practice. Préfontaine and Charbonneau were moving toward a more revolutionary way of working and got closer to their goal by creating the Colonie Artistique de Val-David (a one-of-a-kind arts colony) in the Laurentian mountains north of Montreal, in the summer of 1970.

## Cultural Animation

Founded in 1964 by art critic Yves Robillard and engraver Richard Lacroix, the Fusion des Arts group was a precursor to Jazz Libre insofar as its stated goal was to transform daily life through public creative action. The work these two artists did, along with their colleagues (painter Henry Saxe, sculptor François Soucy, and multi-talented visual artist André Montpetit, to name but a few), echoed the way *Parti pris* sought to appropriate the writings of Henri Lefebvre on the need for a critique of everyday life, and of Guy Debord on the necessity of cultural revolution. In the arena of the arts, Fusion des Arts wanted to apply the strategies of awareness building, communication, and participation that citizens' committees and collectives were deploying through social animation in the Quebec of the 1960s. Its aim was not explicitly leftist; mostly, it wanted to offer solutions to the issue of the democratization of culture raised by the makers of the Quiet Revolution as they rethought the role of the state.

Fusion des Arts put forward a completely new program. They intended to knock down the barriers between its members' art forms and bring them outside galleries and museums. In their 1965 manifesto, the group called for the "socialization of art" through the creation of collective "total works." They refused to "relegate [art] to the sphere of an occasional leisure activity" by separating it "from other social activities an individual might engage in."[2] The group did not stop at simply denouncing bourgeois concepts of culture. It called for the active participation of audiences and consumers as a way of encouraging them to rethink their relation to the cultural productions around them. Robillard and his colleagues knew that actions were often more important than words. They created a moving installation in the lobby of Loew's cinema during the Seventh Montreal International Film Festival (mobiles made of plates upon which the public could draw) and contributed to Expo 67 with unusual instruments activated by the audience, solidifying the collective's iconoclastic status in the process.

Despite its agent provocateur appearance, Fusion des Arts was above all an artists' association that latched on to the social energies created by the Quiet Revolution. They wanted to emphasize the arts in the building of a modern Quebec. Their quest for recognition would succeed through cultural democracy and a redefinition of artists' role in society, as well as their relations with their audiences (in the know or otherwise) and the institutions they depended on to finance and distribute their works (total, participative, and subversive, even underground or countercultural, according to the criteria of the times). Anithe de Carvalho would comment on this "Quebec artistic neo-avant-garde":

> The works are [...] utopian, though not totally breaking from the world as it is—they are not necessarily revolutionary from a political point of view—but the new spaces artworks can inhabit allow for the voice of people uninitiated to the art-world to be heard. These artists and their productions are accepted by institutions, since they question the borders of the art field, but go no further. [...] By getting involved in changing people's living conditions through art, and doing so outside of art institutions, these experiments are carried out in a new realm of practices, though authorized and funded by those institutions.[3]

With perspective, Richard Lacroix would concede that he and his group "were not revolutionaries, just people who were curious, young artists open to what was happening."[4]

All the same, some factions did radicalize as the collective expanded, recruiting new voices and setting up study and action groups. Among the latter was the Comité d'Information Politique, charged with making audiences aware of the need to discuss the "demands of true revolutionary action."[5] An autonomous, self-financing entity, this outgrowth of the Fusion des Arts group raised funds to help defend the Vallières-Gagnon cause, organized two political film festivals, and coordinated a lecture on Marxist aesthetics by French philosopher Alain Badiou. Another subdivision, the Technique d'Action Sociale unit, set out to study in detail, and critically, social and cultural animation efforts in Quebec. It worked on the relevance of "militant action" in the arts and the pressing need for creators to take part in "the national liberation struggle" by establishing, among other things, parallel information and action networks.[6]

The members of Jazz Libre were drawn to this movement, since it proposed a new approach to culture, stressing the idea of social involvement. They saw parallels with their idea of music action, and they were not mistaken. During their meetings, members of the Technique d'Action Sociale unit referred to Jazz Libre's participative way of working and its network-building ability. They asked Préfontaine for help in writing up a workbook for the spring of 1969. Doc authored a text describing his experience with cultural animation:

> The music we play is liberation; it is liberated music. We can't do otherwise than liberate people. Especially if they are aware of what's happening,

> what we're doing, if they're looking into communication techniques instead of searching for a theme and variations.[7]

Préfontaine was perfectly aware that free jazz was difficult music to listen to, but he firmly believed that collective improvisation was a vector of liberation. "In the right situation, I am sure that 90% of young people will open their ears," he added.[8] Jazz Libre had been working to create just those conditions since the band left The Barrel.

At the Association Espagnole, the quartet fraternized with Serge Lemoyne, the "post-Automatist" artist, signatory of Zirmate's *Manifeste infra*, and key member of the Fusion des Arts group. Launched at the end of January 1968, his series of forty "events" was aimed at creating communication channels outside of art galleries and museums to foster community and improve understanding among people so they would be moved to "change their everyday lives."[9] From January 26 to February 4, Jazz Libre took part in event 1 (and 1.5) with actors Philippe Gingras (alias Baron Filip) and Monique Paradis. Entitled *L'Art de manger* ("the art of eating"), this anti-show turned the Association Espagnole into an experimental theatre where visual projections, music, and stage work became integral parts of the experience of eating and—of course—drinking. The quartet then moved on to Acton Vale in the Eastern Townships for events 21 to 24, the numbering system corresponding to the four days of the duration of the program, an eclectic cultural happening that Lemoyne had prepared for his hometown on Saint-Jean-Baptiste Day (Quebec's national holiday, celebrated on June 24).

Jazz Libre was asked to close out the evening of June 23, hitting the stage to the glow of the traditional bonfire.

Buoyed by the experience, the group considered further collaborations with the inner circle of Fusion des Arts, hoping to expand its music action beyond the venues where it was usually played. Préfontaine told Emmanuel Cocke, "We need to meet more people than the ones we know in the places we work. It's about social involvement, involvement with the left."[10] Which was why he wanted to cooperate with Lacroix to create an immersive event where musicians and their audiences would control mobile musical sculptures. It was a "floating project" that would never come to be.[11] Jazz Libre had more success with the cultural action it was working on with Françoise Graham and Iolande Rossignol. The latter was running workshops for children as part of Fusion des Arts, using methods developed by the German composer Carl Orff to bring musical creativity to very young people—interactive exercises centred on the participants and their openness to improvisation. Jazz Libre's idea, with Graham and Rossignol, was to increase young people's awareness of art. "Contrary to public belief, artistic creation is not the privilege of a minuscule minority who went to art school," said their project's description.[12] The music and movement workshops, directed by Rossignol and Graham respectively, were designed to produce a public collective creation. Meanwhile, Jazz Libre was mandated to provide the musical backup and encourage young people in their explorations.

The response to the program was positive. *Jonquière*, a short film by Fernand Dansereau from 1969, showed as much. The film aired on Radio-Canada's *Cent millions de jeunes* on April 11, 1970, and focused on the work accomplished at the Centre Culturel Confédératif in Jonquière, in Quebec's Saguenay region, that previous summer. Rossignol, Graham, and Jazz Libre were accompanied by pianist Pierre Nadeau and coordinator Guy Beaugrand-Champagne. Some forty teenagers had signed up for the music and movement workshops whose aim was "to involve as little didactic teaching as possible and encourage the participants' improvisation abilities to the fullest."[13] The workshops were spread over two days and culminated in an improvised performance at a local college. The young people sang, danced, beat drums, put on sketches, and urged the audience to join them in a climate of experimentation that owed much to the happenings of the times. Jazz Libre intervened throughout the evening with its own style of music, inviting the young performers to join them. Once the adventure was over, one participant explained how he "became aware of sound [...] that instinctively creates inner movement." A powerful education experience "that won't stop here," another person agreed. "Maybe, aesthetically, it wasn't a great piece of creation, but for us, we loved it," added a teenage girl.[14] For her, the experience validated the idea that collective improvisation helped integrate and create cohesion within groups of people.

## The Concert Forum

These events were similar to the concert forums that Jazz Libre started producing in the winter of 1968. The form was simple: first, the group initiated the audience into free jazz by offering short improvisations followed by explanations about its history. A discussion followed, with the audience urged to consider the social impact of jazz. The evening would end with a session of collective improvisation, with the audience sitting in. Jazz Libre played concert forums at Rosemont and Maisonneuve colleges, at McGill University, the Centre de Transition at the Université du Québec (where aspiring teachers transferred to university from the normal school in which they were enrolled), and the Cultural Centre at the University of Sherbrooke. It also took to the stage at the Gesù hall as part of the Semaine de l'Indépendance du Collège Sainte-Marie ("independence week") and accepted invitations from the organizing committee of the winter carnival at the Université de Montréal, as well as similar offers from the student associations at the Collège de Victoriaville and Montreal's school of fine arts, just before its incorporation into Université du Québec à Montréal (UQAM). As a journalist in the student paper *Quartier latin* explained, these concert forums gave young people a chance to discover free jazz while discussing "music, liberation, creation, new ways of living, and everyone's relationship with the world."[15]

Jazz Libre had been considering a Quebec tour of concert forums even before getting involved in *Osstidcho*. Not knowing it would end up accompanying Charlebois and his gang for the next several months, the quartet applied for a grant from the Ministry of Cultural Affairs just prior to the first show at the Théâtre de Quat'sous. Préfontaine hoped to pick up the necessary support for a summer tour of cultural centres in the province. The project he submitted was based on the concert forum concept, with lights and projections added. In the use of a "colour organ," he saw the solution to the problem of sensory overload that he associated with psychedelic projections.[16] The intriguing mechanism he had in mind was composed of a stroboscope, four projectors, and the same number of microphones hooked up to a console. More than 300 slides—photos of musicians, abstract images, and thematic illustrations (about war, the environment, and human relations)—could move across a screen following the rhythm and volume of the music. The group also planned to acquire a number of percussion instruments designed by Orff, similar to the ones employed by Rossignol in her workshops. Unfortunately, his request for funds got bogged down in ministerial bureaucracy, despite Préfontaine's attempts to convince people in the Ministry of Cultural Affairs and the Fédération des Centres Culturels (FCC) that the project was valid.

This failure took the four musicians aback; they were convinced of their music's social value. In a letter addressed to Gilbert Comtois, the director of the FCC, Préfontaine expressed his dismay over the obstacles the group encountered "within the only state organisms in the position to support it," especially since every concert forum presented that spring "was a total and unexpected success, so much so that it was not easy to end the evenings, even after three or four encores."[17] Doc was exaggerating, of course, when it came to young people's enthusiasm for free jazz. Still, Jazz Libre awoke their curiosity. Jacques Valois, whom the group turned to in 1969 and 1970 to replace Maurice Richard, remembered a morning performance in a school—an experience both difficult, due to the group's penchant for nightlife, and fascinating, considering the students' open-mindedness and curiosity.[18] Diane Dupuis, the sound engineer and Préfontaine's partner at the time, also had good memories of the concert forums. The young audience kept "an open mind," but at the same time they wanted to know, "Do you think this is really Quebec music?"[19] "Does the word 'music' really apply?" "If it's just sounds, why do you call it jazz, because, after all, jazz is music?"[20]

Jazz Libre faced a double challenge. It had to justify its appropriation of an African American idiom, then explain to the uninitiated why its collective improvisations really were music. The group's sounds were clearly disconcerting. They had no structure and contained very few themes to hold on to. The solos were executed simultaneously and in discord with the harmonic progressions of traditional jazz, and the polyrhythms were anything but danceable. Préfontaine was aware of those difficulties. At a concert forum at a youth centre in Drummondville, east of Montreal, he explained that the audience had to surrender to the music, despite the sense of "insecurity" it brought, and not look for direction:

> That's the only thing you can do, just follow the musicians' way of communicating and not try and find themes or songs you might know, or blues chords that are dear to you, and all those clichés we have in our minds because we're conditioned by this fucken disgusting commercialized culture. We've got to free ourselves from it, that's what we're trying to do, and we're sure we can get that

across to people, so if you don't mind we're going to play you a little tune, very very free. The musicians haven't made up their minds ahead of time, except just to listen to each other and play together [...], and communicate.[21]

The young people were willing to listen and debate, even if they did not necessarily understand what Jazz Libre was after. It was a time of exploration and experimentation.

The quartet also took the trouble to explain that Quebeckers' cultural and political situation predisposed them to free jazz. The group was echoing the *Parti pris* idea according to which the anti-capitalist and anti-imperialist struggles of the "colonized French Canadians" brought them closer to their African American counterparts. "But our music isn't an imitation of Black free jazz," Préfontaine pointed out.[22] Jazz Libre had no choice but to be *Québécois*, since the group expressed its members' deep cultural roots. "If a Quebecker expresses himself with three other companions [...] I imagine there must be something of Quebec in the sounds they make."[23] By using the French words "Jazz Libre" for the name of the band, the group was not just translating from English; it was using the language to declare its rootedness in Quebec. Which is why the musicians often turned to traditional jigs and reels for their music, instead of the blues. "That music provides us with themes and states our attachment to the French Canadian territory," Préfontaine explained.[24] His explorations in that direction were not very fruitful, but they did speak of the need to rethink free jazz in an explicitly Quebec way, which he had to do because Vallières's metaphor did not catch on among counterculture youth. The group set out to illustrate the mobilizing power of the music through listening sessions and collective improvisation before and with audiences.

Jazz Libre needed to explain what it was doing to its youthful audiences. For many young people at the beginning of the 1970s, jazz was music from the past, out of touch compared to rock. Rock was at the centre of the counterculture that had started shaking up the United States in the 1960s. It dominated the pages of Montreal magazines like *Mainmise* and *Logos.* Rock was "international music," "a complete sensory experience," and "a limitless esthetic of discovery" that "always demands the audience's participation."[25] As fearless theoreticians of the rock genre, the *Mainmise* writers were not averse to hyperbole when they declared the music to be "the engine of the counterculture," describing it as "the synthesis of all contemporary artistic and intellectual movements."[26] *Logos* praised it as "the most vibrant art form in the world today."[27] That enthusiasm displayed the generation's love for groups like Jefferson Airplane, Big Brother and the Holding Company, and The Grateful Dead. These publications insisted that only rock could provide form and force for the new utopias. It was both the engine and the soundtrack of an alternative Quebec that counterculture young people were questing after.

With its print run of more than 20,000 copies, *Mainmise* was required reading for the youth movement. No surprise, then, that Jazz Libre was having trouble getting its message across without the backup of Charlebois or L'Infonie. The magazine's editorial board did add the music of the Modern Jazz Quartet to the list of records to listen to while consuming recreational drugs. And it did include several jazz albums in its columns, notably *The Music of the Frontiersman*.[28] But the inspiration wasn't there, and it lifted the titles from a jazz column that Richard Thérien started publishing in 1973. This brave effort lasted only a few issues and ended with an eight-page text entitled "What is Jazz?"[29] That kind of overview could never situate free jazz in the protest movements that were moving through the Western world in the 1960s and 1970s. To make matters worse, Thérien accorded only one paragraph to local music. As for Jazz Libre, he simply noted that the group had contributed "to the renewal of Quebec jazz."[30]

The fleeting interest given to free jazz also proved that it was not easy to co-opt it, as opposed to rock. The silence that surrounded it may have been the result of the fact that the first work to study the counterculture included neither young African American militants nor their cultural production. Published in 1969, *The Making of a Counter Culture* essentially looked into white middle-class youth in the United States and their revolt against their parents' technocratic, bourgeois culture. The author of the book, Theodore Roszak, circumscribed the points of resistance (and their corresponding soundtracks) that could be linked to the notion of counterculture. This way of seeing was quickly adopted by others. Yet white youth in North America were not working in a vacuum, and their movements intersected with those of young African Americans on the nation's campuses and in the streets during demonstrations against the Vietnam War. The music young people were listening to was inspired, at times, by free jazz. Think of records like Frank Zappa's *Uncle Meat* or *Kick Out the Jams* (featuring Sun Ra) by the MC5, both issued in 1969. Released around the same time, the efforts of Charlebois and L'Infonie with Jazz Libre did not really do much better in terms of changing mindsets in Quebec; people also did not think of the counterculture as anything more than a hippie movement.

Préfontaine and Charbonneau left L'Infonie with the intention of making their free jazz heard. They used language designed to be understood by counterculture magazines. Their music action was based on the idea that the inner revolution did not need to take precedence over any other movement. Doc maintained that "true collective improvisation" was a way of reconciling the individual and the collective self. This musical practice would encourage new experiences in communication, and from them would emerge true political and social consciousness: "[From] this point of view, free jazz is part of the current effort to resist falling into ranks, and being slaves to the machine, and standardization." Free jazz could also "touch the sublime"; rock had nothing on it.[31]

Jazz Libre's attempts to get its music heard were accompanied by a critique of Quebec's love affair with rock. Doc was concerned that a number of emerging groups were happy simply to imitate their neighbours to the south:

> It's sad to see and absolutely painful to hear!!! [...] because they're all doing the same thing. Young people are learning how to make music by listening to American records, and writing songs

> in English. [...] Without knowing it, they are sabotaging their creativity and their culture from the start, they're co-opted, colonized, like French-speaking Quebeckers who talk English together.[32]

That does not mean that Jazz Libre was against that musical genre. Préfontaine and his bandmates were aware that rock, like jazz, helped underscore Quebec's place in North America, its *américanité*. But they believed that vigilance was required to avoid cultural colonialism and the co-opting of alternative movements. Which was why they applauded Charlebois and groups like La Révolution Française and Dionysos who were promoting French-language, made-in-Quebec rock.

The growing popularity of pop festivals and the sky-rocketing costs associated with these events created concern as well. In the summer of 1970, after the announcement of a concert at the Autostade in Montreal featuring The Band, Janis Joplin, and the Ginger Baker Airforce, *Logos* denounced the way opportunistic promoters were co-opting the counterculture.[33] And *Mainmise* published an article about the Rock Liberation Front, a New York association that set out to preserve the integrity of young people's cultural events. "The Rock Liberation Front is dedicated to recovering the essence of rock: participation, understanding, fun, peace, and happiness." The author stressed the need to set up workshops and seminars on the music, promote audience participation, and reduce ticket prices. "It's time to denounce the rock profit-takers."[34]

## The Val-David Arts Colony

By the time those articles came out in *Logos* and *Mainmise*, Jazz Libre already had its own plan. At the beginning of summer 1970, it created an arts colony in Val-David, a Laurentian town an hour north of Montreal, to offer young people an alternative to expensive rock concerts with its own cultural events, all in one place and over a longer period of time. Open "25 hours a day from June 25 to September 25," the goal of this self-governing project was to "demystify art" and "popularize it and make it accessible to everyone."[35] The group sought support from the FCC and other organizations working with young people to help convince them to visit the banks of the Rivière du Nord, where everything was happening.

All summer long, Jazz Libre and a number of volunteers kept the music workshops going, adding poetry, sculpture, and painting. Most of the organizers lived communally in the cottage on site. The rest pitched their tents where they could. "We'll cook wild food. We'll build a collective bread oven. Come pitch your tent or build your hut next to ours," ran their invitation.[36] Françoise Labonne, Charbonneau's partner at the time, would later describe the adventure as "a big peace and love fiesta."[37] The colourful posters that Jazz Libre printed for the occasion reflected that state of mind. The image: two naked figures walking toward a sunny planet Earth. Musical notes soared toward other planets, and rays of light formed a rainbow that spelled out "LA COLONIE ARTISTIQUE DE VAL-DAVID."[38]

Meanwhile, Jazz Libre needed a new drummer to bring the project to fruition. Guy Thouin had left the group, and the three remaining band members hired Cyril Lepage after watching him play in Old Montreal. Lepage was born in Rimouski in 1933 and learned drums and guitar by accompanying popular bands in the hotels and dance clubs of the Lower Saint Lawrence region. He discovered talents as a jazzman he did not know he had when Montreal musicians passing through Rimouski found themselves without a drummer. He joined them and began a career that would take him to Montreal in the middle of the 1960s. Like many musicians, he accompanied various singers, both pop and folk, gave music lessons, and perfected his theory and technique, auditioning for the best contracts to keep the wolf from the door. Lepage knew very little about Jazz Libre but decided to join them anyway, hoping that a stay in Val-David would be a kind of vacation.

He was a worthy candidate, since he had some experience with avant-garde jazz. He even told a journalist from his native region that he had gotten more interested in "progressive, free jazz" since he had arrived in Montreal, thanks to his musical explorations with guitarist Sonny Greenwich and bassist Freddy McHugh.[39] Lepage also shared the stage with Valois, continuing the free jazz adventure that the latter had begun with Walter Boudreau during Expo 67. Lepage saw avant-garde jazz as a way to breathe new life into his music; his interests were above all aesthetic, though he was ready to join the spirit of Jazz Libre's music action as part of the group's many concert forums. He was an integral part of the discussions with the audiences and referred to his confreres as "poets in rebellion." During a show in a rural region, he explained that their music had to be distinguished from American free jazz. "We have our revolt, too, and we're going to express it through our own jazz."[40] For Lepage, the group's collective improvisations were an opportunity to throw off the alienating working conditions that showbiz foisted on jazz musicians. The honeymoon did not last long, since he did not fully endorse Jazz Libre's political program. Neither did he fit in with the anarchy of the arts colony, especially when the finances were not enough for the four musicians' needs.

Lepage left just as the group was preparing a four-day event to close out the season and celebrate Labour Day. Jazz Libre hurriedly turned to Curly Virgil, a drummer in his thirties who had met Préfontaine at the beginning of the 1960s. The reconstituted quartet intended to put on a real party for the young audience who had been buffeted by the fiasco that was the Woodstock Pop Festival in Manseau, in rural central Quebec. Organized a month earlier by Woods Production, with advice from Michael Lang, the founder of the already legendary Woodstock Music & Air Fair that had taken place in New York state the year before, the Manseau pop festival was to bring together the biggest names in rock over the July 31 weekend. The high ticket prices were criticized by demonstrators determined to protest the theft of the counterculture. Of the 150,000 concertgoers expected, only 15,000 took the trouble to travel to Manseau. The internationally renowned groups were also missing in action; only Dr. John the Night Tripper made the trip. Heavy rain, invasive surveillance (from the police, medical officials, and journalists), numerous overdoses, and a succession of unknown bands, interspersed with recorded music and impromptu acts, were more than enough to discourage the audience. The promoters lost some $125,000 in this painful failure.

In this context, Jazz Libre's "people's party" took on an obvious political flavour, since it presented itself as the real alternative to the utopias of counterculture youth. The group intended to spend no more than $50 for its "anti-capitalist pop festival."[41] The event was to take place from September 4 to 7, and everything would be free. Préfontaine, Charbonneau, Richard, Virgil, and their other partners at the arts colony knew they could count on rock groups like Dionysos and Nouvelles Frontières. Members of the Mouvement de Libération du Taxi, the Front de Libération Populaire, and the Front d'Action Politique supported the quartet and their comrades. This one-time convergence around Jazz Libre spoke volumes about the work accomplished over the summer. An article published in the first and only issue of the radical paper *La Claque* ("the slap") explained that "the summer has been a build-up, a sort of social movement [...] toward society's natural breakup and renewal as a solid, united front." The author added, "Anything can happen on Labour Day weekend. Like a real pop fest. Just show up [...] at the hippie campground, as people around here call it. Man, if they knew."[42] There is no byline, but the author was most probably Pol Chantraine. He was responsible, along with Pierre Vallières, for part of the publication's editorial content. He was also one of the people organizing the activities in Val-David.

This "anti-capitalist pop festival" quickly attracted the forces of law and order. The Sûreté du Quebec (Quebec Provincial Police, QPP) found out about the event by reading *Journal de Montréal*, a daily tabloid. The force got worried about the presence in Val-David of young people "known to be involved in narcotics [and] organizing sexual orgies of all kinds."[43] The Woodstock Pop Festival in Manseau had given QPP agents the opportunity to observe the excesses of young people up close. Some officers had infiltrated the festivalgoers undercover. Corporal Jean-Luc Paquin and officer Roger Hovington witnessed how easily recreational drugs circulated. In their report, they noted the "deleterious effects" of such a crowd when it came to morality, but also public health.[44] Captain Robert Turpin backed up the findings, adding that, in Manseau, he had seen "deplorable scenes of uncleanliness, exposure, nudity, reckless and unrestricted consumption of alcoholic beverages and drugs as well as the open and public sale of those drugs."[45] The QPP officers had their eyes trained on Val-David during the lead-up to Jazz Libre's festival.

The arts colony site was under special surveillance. The police forces involved noted that the local government had not issued a permit for the event. André Séguin, Val-David's town secretary, refused to authorize "a festival on this site because of the lack of organization, planning, hygiene, and the bad reputation of the people who spend time at the arts colony."[46] Officer Michel Laberge wrote up this résumé of the situation in his report: the organizers cannot ensure the presence of security or medical staff; the site does not conform to the hygiene standards of the Ministry of Health since there are no showers or public toilets; and the only restaurant on site could lose its licence because of unsanitary conditions. Laberge anticipated a situation similar to the one observed by his colleagues in Manseau. He based his conclusions on a report completed earlier in August, after a visit to Val-David:

> It seems obvious that at this place there are people distributing narcotics and drugs, and on weekends there are shows in a barn, with scenes of nudity and indecent actions, and besides marijuana cigarettes are being smoked regularly, and Hashish, and people are taking Mesculin or other pills [*sic*].[47]

A search of the site for illicit substances turned up nothing. In the end, the authorities chose not to cancel the festival. Instead, they would keep it under control and surveillance.

The organizers protested not only the surveillance but the repression they claimed they were victims of. On Friday, September 4, the day after Laberge's unscheduled visit, Chantraine and Charbonneau gave a press conference at the Association Espagnole. The latter said this to the journalists there:

> We're leftists and the police keep harassing us. It's been going on for a while. There were two raids this week, up at the arts campground. The police [...] are hoping to find drugs at our place. Each time, they did not find anything.[48]

The QPP made no arrests and found no illicit substances, but it did seize "revolutionary newspapers, and a tape of a Black Panthers meeting in the United States."[49] Concerned at first by the festival's counterculture character, QPP officers finally took note of the arts colony's leftist orientation.

For the organizers, this "anti-capitalist pop festival" was a success. More than 3,000 young people attended rock shows by groups like Dionysos, Levant, Smack, Nouvelles Frontières, and O'Cannabis. Jazz Libre had its time on the stage too. Préfontaine summed it up this way:

> Everyone cooperated, they paid attention to the organizers and avoided taking "hard" drugs [...] that could have caused bad trips. There were as many people as at Manseau [...] and not a single bad trip, compared to 600 at Manseau. And we didn't have a budget of a quarter-million dollars, a security force that cost $45,000, and a $20,000 sound system, with American bands at top prices.[50]

The whole event cost Jazz Libre a little under $200. "We beat the buck," exclaimed Doc.[51] Charbonneau was also proud of the work accomplished, considering that Val-David, like the group's music, was "improvised from start to finish."[52] Most of all, he was happy about how the participants reacted. "The kids were with us, it was amazing," he told the editorial board of *Quartier latin*.[53]

***

Préfontaine and Charbonneau wanted to do more to expand their music action beyond the usual places where Quebec youth gathered. "We want workers to come, too, and think it's cool."[54] Jazz Libre's idea of cultural practice aimed for a true transformation of everyday life, both work and leisure. Organizing an "anti-capitalist pop festival" in Val-David over the Labour Day weekend was a step in that direction. By trying to place its music in the context of class struggle, the group displayed its fidelity to the left-wing, revolutionary independence movement. The connections it made and the experience it built up moving from The Barrel to the Association Espagnole pointed to the direction its music was heading in. At the same time, those connections completely cut the group off from the Montreal jazz scene. In fact, the quartet scarcely had any contact with it at all by then. The Val-David arts colony was a turning point in Jazz Libre's search for revolutionary practice. Préfontaine and Charbonneau met FLQ members Paul Rose and Francis Simard there, and together they agreed to create something completely new: a socialist commune in the Eastern Townships.

[4]

# Free Improv for Communal Living
## (1970–1973)

*It's not every day that a bunch of well-known musicians devote themselves to social and political action. But that's exactly what Jazz Libre du Québec did yesterday, at the headquarters of the [trade union federation] CSN, by launching a fund-raising campaign to enable the group to buy and organize "Petit Québec Libre," a rural communal property.*[1]

–Jean Basile

"LET'S NOT WASTE OUR TIME AND ESPECIALLY NOT OUR PRECIOUS VACATIONS," read the tract that Jazz Libre was handing out in union circles the year following the group's experience at Val-David.[2] Vacations must be "politically useful," so said the flyer whose mission was to advertise the existence of Petit Québec Libre (literally, "little free Quebec"), a rural commune that styled itself as the microcosm of a future greater free Quebec, French-speaking and socialist.[3] Officially launched at winter's end, 1971, the project found its inspiration in the group's musical experiments—in the relations between individuals created by collective improvisation. Jean Préfontaine and his band had no intention of seeking refuge in a parallel society like the young hippies who were heading back to the land. Quite the opposite. They wanted to revise and improve their cultural action and bring together the different strands of the movement that opposed the powers in place.

This common front would depend on Jazz Libre's ability to turn its music action into a vector for communication, organization, and participation. It would attempt to mobilize a wide swath of Quebec leftists, from student militants to FLQ members, along with unionists, Marxist-Leninists, Maoists, and radical feminists. Its main objective was to "create the necessary conditions to build revolutionary organization in Quebec, [and] to fight spontaneism, reformism, and the separation of theory and practice."[4]

As I will show in this chapter, Jazz Libre succeeded in turning its music into revolutionary practice through the commune. However, the group's resolute move toward the radical leftist nationalist factions in the wake of the October Crisis would make Petit Québec Libre the preferred target of the police forces charged with wiping out FLQ terrorism and discouraging its sympathizers, both real and presumed.

## Genesis

Jean Préfontaine and Yves Charbonneau first met FLQ members Paul Rose and Francis Simard at the Val-David arts colony at the end of the summer of 1970. At that point, the two musicians decided to move a hundred kilometres east of Montreal, to the intersection of Concession Roads 9 and 11, near the village of Sainte-Anne-de-la-Rochelle, in the Eastern Townships. Rose had bought a farm there several years earlier as a place for the FLQ to gather. The RCMP discovered this hideout during an antiterrorism operation on June 22, 1970, in Prévost in the Lower Laurentians. Officers from the QPP arrived at Sainte-Anne-de-la-Rochelle the next day, but they arrested no one, since they did not recognize Simard (he had supplied them with a false name) and did not find Rose (he had hidden in the attic). Mindful that they could no longer use the property for fear of further police raids, the two FLQ militants decided to rent the farm to Jazz Libre after seeing how serious the group was in Val-David. They had only two conditions: Préfontaine and Charbonneau were to turn the site into a "a centre for political action" where the activities and services would be "free of charge."[5] The musicians agreed wholeheartedly and were already hard at work in late September 1970. Maurice Richard wasted no time joining them.[6]

Using their experience from Val-David, the trio immediately chose a communal model of organization. They were simply continuing what Jazz Libre had been doing since its beginnings in 1967, when the group lived as a proto-commune, setting down the basis of their music action. "You can't play revolutionary music and live like a fucking bourgeois," Charbonneau explained. "The group lives the way it plays. We communicate in total freedom and the only criterion is responsibility," he added. Préfontaine agreed:

> When you try to free yourself, you always find something new. You drop musical structures and trust the four musicians, the ability to

> spontaneously invent ways of playing together that will lead to unity. Starting with every person's total freedom, trusting each person's creativity, we were able to communicate among ourselves and create new music that was always changing. [...] It's normal, when you're having musical experiences like that, that they'll influence your human relations, and you want to bring them into your day-to-day life.[7]

The lessons learned through improvised music motivated them to continue their work at Petit Québec Libre. When it came to organizing and administering the commune, the process was similar to their musical collective. All decisions were made as a group after lengthy discussion to reconcile individual and collective voices.

The size of Petit Québec Libre, some 1.75 square kilometres, situated on either side of Concession Road 9, allowed Jazz Libre to give free rein to its imagination, and the group set about converting the farm into a centre for political action. The site included two maple groves and a sugar shack, a stable, an orchard, a repair shop, as well as a barn to be made into a conference room and music hall. Renovated, the former pigsty was now a reception area and information centre. Préfontaine and Diane Dupuis set up a Gestetner press there that would produce the commune's newspaper and print tracts and posters. A large campground and daycare could accommodate workers' families who might want to spend their vacations with the commune's inhabitants (some twenty in all), who pooled their skills and revenues (payments for shows, salaries, family benefits, unemployment insurance, etc.) so everything would be free on the site. The official opening was the kick-off for "OPERATION FUCK THE BUCK."[8]

Jazz Libre designed the space with its cultural animation projects in mind. It offered workshops (music, theatre, poetry, and sculpture) with the goal of forging "conditions that will encourage people to become aware of their ability to creatively engage in the arts."[9] Poet and sculptor Jean Gauguet-Larouche, visual artist Lise Landry, and actress Marie-Claire Nolin from the Théâtre Radical du Québec all volunteered their time. The group staged "evenings of comradeship," with various speakers debating current events.[10] Political films were screened—among them, *La bataille d'Alger* (*The Battle of Algiers*, Gilles Pontecorvo, 1966), *Taire des hommes* (Pascal Gélinas and Pierre Harel, 1968), and *On est au cotton* (*Cotton Mill, Treadmill*, Denys Arcand, 1976)—which were meant to lead to further discussion.[11] The commune dwellers wanted to provide people with ways of expressing themselves through artistic activities. They expected the participants to then develop the desire to liberate themselves in their daily lives. The cultural programming was subversive in that it offered a critique of Quebec's cultural, economic, and political situation. In the end, the goal was "the political stimulation of the campers" in hopes of creating a consensus around the national question.[12] Petit Québec Libre was meant to be the microcosm of a future socialist and independent Quebec.

Revolutionary action required complete engagement; Préfontaine and Charbonneau invested all their energy in the project. The commune monopolized their time during the first year, and Jazz Libre had to reduce its musical output.

Richard was unhappy; he stepped away from the group and returned to Montreal in the winter of 1971 to embark on other undertakings. The two hornmen announced that the group was breaking up and that a new ensemble was coming together that would include all the members of the commune. "Jazz Libre is dead! Long live the members of Petit Québec Libre!" Actually, Jazz Libre did not cease its activities, except that now it had to hire musicians if it wanted to give concerts outside of the commune. Several times a week, Doc and Charbonneau invited the young and not-so-young, women and men, commune dwellers and visitors, musicians and non-musicians, to join improv sessions to help pave the way for an independent Quebec, a process that demanded the ability to invent and communicate together. The two horn players were convinced that their music was "for the people" because everyone could play it and it was collective.[13] But then there was the issue of whether it was listenable. In any case, they saw it as a way of mobilizing the Quebec working class.

## Communion

After their Val-David experience, Préfontaine and Charbonneau chose to focus on workers' families to make their music action into a true revolutionary praxis. In search of solid foundations for the commune, they wrote to François Mario Bachand, an FLQ member in exile in Paris since 1969. The musicians wanted his advice about organization and recruitment. In a letter dated March 19, 1971, Bachand stated that the commune should avoid at all costs becoming a refuge for "petty bourgeois intellectuals" from Outremont (an upscale, French-speaking district of Montreal). "Make sure you recruit a solid base of sons and daughters of workers." The workers of Quebec had to be organized and brought together, supported "by all means, including gifts of maple syrup," he added with a note of humour that betrayed his homesickness.[14]

Bachand's counsel did not fall on deaf ears. The commune's 1971 manifesto was focused on the "sons and daughters of Quebec workers":

> WE WANT, using our shared experience, to contribute to the collective and individual liberation of the Quebec nation.
>
> WE WANT to inform our compatriots in our own words of our goals, and that PETIT QUÉBEC LIBRE farm is open to all and there to encourage everyone's creative expression. [...]
>
> WE BELIEVE that the distrust, denunciation, and collective guilt created by the media, and the incomprehension and petty squabbles between groups, must rapidly disappear and give way to solidarity.
>
> WE WANT, through our own means and with the help of other patriots, PETIT QUÉBEC LIBRE to become the place of all Quebec workers, their property, and their collective accomplishment.[15]

The commune dwellers distributed thousands of copies of the manifesto across the province.

They also launched a newspaper called *Le P'tit Québec libre* to promote their ideas to working-class families.[16] With a 3,000-copy print run, the publication informed people about what the commune was up to and told the readership about the "situation of workers in Quebec, their cultural, social, political, and economic status."[17] The paper presented a synthesis of Marxist theories about class struggle and denounced exploitation in all its forms. Its editorial board gave its support to, among others, the employees of the Valcourt Bombardier plant and those of Montrose Worsted in Granby, two Eastern Townships factories. It offered advice about how to organize and reminded workers that the cooperative model, though constructive, was only a partial solution to the "toppling of the capitalist system."[18] For the strikers, it listed their "rights and responsibilities in case of arrest."[19] In language that was sometimes crude, not beating around the bush, the editorial board denounced English imperialism and capitalism:

> Shit, we're all human beings, all the same, we define ourselves that way through our involvement. So much crap in the system… and I think we've all eaten enough of that. […] You've got the choice, you're free! To do what? To work together to create, either that or let injustice grind you down. We, the people of Quebec, you, the Black prisoners in the ghettos sentenced to death by bourgeois tyranny, putting up walls to hide their garbage![20]

Like the FLQ, the Petit Québec Libre commune appropriated the image of the "old patriot of 1837," then transformed him into a worker.[21] But the commune did not condone violence despite its strong language and the connotations of its iconography.

Préfontaine and Charbonneau could count on the support of the Conseil Central des Syndicats Nationaux de Montréal (the CCSNM, a council of unions in the city). On January 26, 1971, in the organization's offices, Jazz Libre launched the "$0$" campaign, aimed at the unions.[22] This was a request for financing to pay the rent (a symbolic amount of $1 a year), the property taxes ($250 a year), and the mortgage (an annual payment of $2,000) on the farm. The CCSNM provided paper for the musicians, printed their documents, and distributed their press releases and tracts. Jazz Libre's 1968 recording and copies of the commune's newspaper were also made available to union members.

Among unionists, support for Jazz Libre was seen as a way of increasing political awareness in workers by promoting cultural democracy. Fernand Foisy, a man close to well-known union leader Michel Chartrand, would explain that the organization had a "favourable prejudice" toward artists like Charbonneau and Préfontaine.[23]

As well as sharing Jazz Libre's desire for an independent, socialist Quebec, the CCSNM believed that art could be useful in political and social struggles. Its executive committee gave particular attention to the cultural interests of Quebec citizens in its Resolution for an Independent Quebec, which echoed the *Parti pris* theories about the double oppression of Quebec workers, and asserted that political domination could not be dissociated from cultural, economic, and social domination.[24] The fourteenth congress of the CCSNM was held during the general strike called by the Front Commun Intersyndical (a common front of unions) in April 1972; it was the occasion to denounce both the "bourgeois culture" of the elites and the "utilitarian culture of the masses."[25] Victor Leroux, in charge of education for the union organization, had noted the previous year, "I don't believe that [Jean] Béliveau, Mack Jones, or Chrysler will be the liberators of the Quebec working class."[26] He was listened to, as shown by the 1972 Declaration of Principles in which the CCSNM promised to pursue its "cultural fight" while "giving free rein to forms of popular expression and communication."[27]

The Théâtre des Travailleurs ("workers' theatre") was an important element in the cultural aspect of the struggle. The CCSNM had been backing the group since 1970.[28] Better known by the name L'Engrenage ("the driving wheels"), this collective was busy preparing the "cultural revolution," striving to increase workers' awareness "by creating [against established cultural power] counterpropaganda and counterculture arising from people's self-expression."[29] Jean-Pierre Compain, Charlotte Boisjoli, and Lise Rose all led workshops in visual and theatre arts; some sixty workers participated in L'Engrenage's collective works. Among them was Patrice Beckerich, one of the "Lapalme guys" recruited for his talents as a percussionist.[30] The group's rehearsal room was provided by the CCSNM. Their creations—pictorial works, poems, and stage plays—were based on the idea that art was "a tool for social change."[31] Jazz Libre and the Théâtre des Travailleurs pursued similar goals. The latter group was set to give a performance at Petit Québec Libre on Saturday, June 24. Beckerich knew the place since he had stayed there with his family earlier in the year after the CCSNM's promotion efforts had reached him.

He fraternized with Préfontaine and decided to join forces with Jazz Libre. They had been without a drummer for a long stretch of time, so the group welcomed this new musician with open arms. He had experience as a militant with "the Lapalme guys" and a percussionist with the Théâtre des Travailleurs. Born in Paris in 1946, Beckerich immigrated to Quebec with his parents at the beginning of the 1950s. He received his first set of drums when he turned fourteen, and went on to form The Roamers, then Les Patriotes, pop music groups that played weekend shows in various hotels and clubs. A member of the Association des Orchestres de Montréal, he went from one contract to the next, finally deciding he needed steady work. He became a truck driver for Lapalme, a company that carried mail in Montreal. Some time later, Eric W. Kierans, postmaster general, declined to renew the contract between his government and the Lapalme company. Beckerich quickly acquainted himself with militant unionism, taking part in the many demonstrations organized by his union local in front of Parliament in Ottawa. During this campaign, that lasted nearly two years, Compain asked him to join the Théâtre des Travailleurs.

This convergence of individuals and groups around Petit Québec Libre created concern after the October Crisis events. That year, 1970, the province faced unprecedented political events. As a reminder of those days, on October 5, the "Libération" cell of the FLQ, led by Jacques Lanctôt, kidnapped British diplomat James R. Cross to put pressure on the federal government. The cell demanded, among other things, the freeing of some twenty political prisoners, a half-million-dollar ransom, the rehiring of the Lapalme workers, and the broadcasting of the FLQ manifesto. The text was read on radio station CKAC, then on TV, on Radio-Canada. As for the rest, the authorities refused to budge, which incited the "Chénier" cell (Bernard Lortie and Francis Simard, along with Paul Rose and his brother Jacques) to stage further action. On October 10, the group kidnapped Pierre Laporte, the labour and immigration minister in Robert Bourassa's provincial government. This led to a state of alert and then to the proclamation of the War Measures Act on October 16. The Canadian Army was seen in the streets of Montreal, and a wave of arrests (more than 500 in all) and searches without warrants (several thousand) was carried out across the province. The discovery of Laporte's body the night of October 17 and 18 created a climate of repression that lasted far past Cross's freeing and the arrest of those responsible for Laporte's death.

These events had a big impact on Préfontaine and Charbonneau, of course, though the previous year had been anything but restful. On February 13, 1969, the FLQ network of student Pierre-Paul Geoffroy set off a bomb at the Montreal Stock Exchange to "strike at the heart of the capitalist system."[32] Arrested several weeks later, Geoffroy pleaded guilty and received 124 life sentences. Another major trial was that of Pierre Bourgault, accused of incitement to riot during the 1968 Saint-Jean-Baptiste parade. The head of the independence-minded RIN had warned there would be violence if Prime Minister Pierre

Elliot Trudeau attended the festivities. Bourgault was acquitted on July 24. Others were not as lucky. The student leaders who, between January 29 and February 11, took part in the occupation of the Sir George Williams University computer centre to denounce the racism to which they were subjected ended up in prison, deported, or exiled after the riot caused by extreme police intervention. David Austin reminds us that "the rebellion at Sir George was not just the largest student occupation in Canadian history, but internationally the most destructive (to property) act of civil disobedience on a university campus."[33] Yet this event did not seem to attract the attention of Préfontaine and Charbonneau. Given that it was related to the Black community and in English-speaking Montreal, it lay outside their field of vision. Their eyes were focused on the international scene (Fidel Castro's Cuba, the Black Panther Party, and Ho Chi Minh) in order to better situate Quebec in decolonizing struggles. This blind spot is important and points to a contradiction. An event like the Sir George Williams occupation showed that Montreal could be "a meeting place for different colonized subjects, a site where they could meet each other and imagine a different future for their countries of origin."[34]

The radicalization of Jazz Libre began at the Association Espagnole, then in Val-David, as the group met *Parti pris* members and FLQ sympathizers. The connection it made with the FLQ was no passing fancy, as shown by Préfontaine and Charbonneau's meetings with Rose and Simard. Ex-FLQ members Gilles Choquette and Jacques Désormeaux lived at Petit Québec Libre. Jean-Luc Arène and Lise Balcer, who were close to the Rose family, also visited the place. As well,

Daniel Waterlot, a former policeman and active member of the Quebec Communist Party (Marxist-Leninist), could also be spotted there. The two horn players hesitated between Trotskyism and Maoism without necessarily settling on one side or the other.[35] Not only did their work in music make all dogma impossible, it was not easy to pick and choose between the various factions. As Jean-Philippe Warren explains, "Before 1975 especially, the list of groups grew and became practically interminable, and even sharp-eyed observers of the times could not always pick their way through the maze of foundations, divisions, unions, break-ups, schisms, and tactical alliances."[36] Given the context, Préfontaine and Charbonneau borrowed from here and there: Marx and Mao Zedong's *Little Red Book* as well as *Parti pris* and *White Niggers of America*. They also dipped into the *Bulletin de liaison* of the Comité Provisoire de Coordination Indépendance-Socialisme, and publications like *Indochine vaincra* (of the committee for solidarity with the people of Indochina), *Sud Vietnam en lutte* (of the central organ of the National Liberation Front of South Vietnam), *Le Patriote* (of the Haitian movement for patriotic action), *Fedayin* (the journal of the Quebec–Palestine Association), and *The National Guardian* (later *The Guardian*, a radical New York newspaper of Maoist inspiration).

Some were sceptical when it came to just how peaceful the commune was. The press wondered about the existence of a "terrorist camp in Sainte-Anne" where a Marxist revolution was being prepared.[37] It was worried about a "new Maison du Pêcheur 60 miles from Montreal," trying to associate Jazz Libre with the youth hostel that Rose had opened in the Gaspé in 1969.[38] The Percé site was seen at the time as the cradle of the FLQ. Alarmed by these reports, Léonel Beaudoin, MP of the Ralliement Créditiste party for the riding of Richmond-Wolfe, asked Prime Minister Trudeau if he was "aware that in Quebec there are youth camps involved in subversive propaganda and in teaching young people how to handle weapons and organize rebellion in the country?"[39] In answer, Trudeau said he knew nothing of such places and urged Beaudoin to communicate all relevant information to Jean-Pierre Goyer, Canada's solicitor general and responsible for the RCMP in its fight against the revolutionary left. But the Mounties already had their eyes trained on Sainte-Anne-de-la-Rochelle in 1971.

Préfontaine and Charbonneau did their best to refute the idea that Petit Québec Libre was a nest of terrorists. Doc was categorical: "There's no dynamite here, no training camp."[40] According to him, terrorism had been a "necessary and sad step" that no longer had a role to play in the Quebec of the 1970s.[41] Charbonneau expressed the same opinion. During a "comradeship evening," he explained that the story of the FLQ was that of "some damned good guys [...] who sacrificed themselves for Quebec [...] because the people weren't ready."[42] He added that it was time to go beyond spontaneism and fully enter the post–October Crisis period, "a period of organization [...] where all Quebeckers have to be aware of what's happening."[43] There was no doubt that the FLQ occupied an important symbolic place in the narrative the commune used to describe its project for nationhood, but its role was that of a precursor—in other words, a historical link in the chain of events leading to the building of a socialist, independent

Quebec. Charbonneau was fighting armed with a trumpet, not a machine gun. The commune informed the MP from Richmond-Wolfe that he was barking up the wrong tree:

> We are inviting Mr. Beaudoin to come and inspect our shock troupes and our well-stocked store of weapons of all kinds: two 22 rifles, an old 20-calibre hunting musket that was fired by a Patriot at the Battle of Saint-Eustache in 1837, picks, shovels, saws, axes, flutes, bongos, bugles, a trumpet, a sax, guitars, a piano, and… work… PLENTY OF IT![44]

The commune attacked journalists for their lack of objectivity. It denounced the heavy hand of the establishment on the media, and tried to counteract the sensationalist coverage of the commune and its inhabitants.[45]

Concerned by its image in the region, the commune insisted it had no intention of disturbing the peace and quiet of Sainte-Anne-de-la-Rochelle and drawing down police repression onto the village. The members left copies of *Le P'tit Québec libre* in the local grocery stores, and their journal made fun of the rumours about the farm's penchant for terrorism and nudity. "It's all Julie's fault (age 2), she likes to walk around without any clothes on. You know what kids are like at her age!"[46] Préfontaine imagined that the local farmers would do business with the hundreds of campers who would stay at the commune in summers to come. As well, he thought, young people from the Townships would want to take advantage of the cultural workshops.[47] The commune dwellers wanted to cultivate good relations with the neighbours by offering free hay and recruiting volunteers to help farmers who needed a hand. A softball team was formed to play against the village's side.[48] All this was meant to help Petit Québec Libre integrate into its environment in hopes of "bringing [...] the rural masses in the region" into the left-wing independence movement.[49]

The commune population liked to point out that the movement toward a free, socialist Quebec was not the exclusive territory of men. They repeatedly stated that a true common front would be possible only with the active participation of women from all sectors of society. And they had an example: the Front Commun des Québécoises (FCQ) that arose spontaneously in 1969. During one of the discussion sessions at the commune, Préfontaine lauded the heroism of the women who mobilized in Montreal on November 28, 1969, to challenge Mayor Jean Drapeau's "anti-demonstration" bylaw.[50] The FCQ was the predecessor of the Front de Libération des Femmes du Québec (FLFQ), founded several weeks later. The FCQ's first initiative was a reminder to everyone that there is strength in union, and that whatever the different levels of government might undertake, it will always be insufficient. The advice coming from Petit Québec Libre's publication concerning organization and the rights of the proletariat was directed to men and women alike. The commune stated its support for the female workers of World Wide Gum in Granby, also in the Eastern Townships, in their struggle with their bosses. The employees were invited to the farm to network, get informed, or simply relax.

The commune furthered its mobilization efforts in the summer of 1971 by supporting Lise Balcer, who was found guilty of contempt of court for refusing to testify in the Rose trial. Balcer was protesting against the rule that forbade women from being jury members. *Le P'tit Québec libre* reproduced a long excerpt from a conversation she had with the magazine *Point de mire*, earlier in March. The militant discussed her prison experiences and the social conditions that oppressed woman. She also included a harsh critique of male intellectuals who were calling for socialist revolution:

> Guys from the left are fighting against one type of exploitation, but when it comes to women, they're on the wrong side. A real revolutionary fights against all forms of oppression, no matter what they are.[51]

The commune was impatiently awaiting the return of their comrade "temporarily on the sidelines in Tanguay prison" since the beginning of the spring.[52] A rapprochement seemed possible between radical feminism and leftist nationalism, despite the persistence of male chauvinism in Quebec's political culture of the times.

In addition to the efforts described, the commune population studied the FLFQ's strategies to make left-wing nationalists aware that women's liberation could not be separated from that of the Quebec nation and the working class. "LONG LIVE WOMEN'S LIBERATION FRONTS AND ALL POWER TO THE PEOPLE," the commune exclaimed, backing the FLFQ's militants.[53] Seven of them found themselves behind bars with Balcer in 1971. They had been sentenced to several weeks in prison for contempt of court. Marjolaine Péloquin, Louise Toupin, Nicole Dostie, Francine Aubin, Nicole Therrien, Arlette Rouleau, and Micheline Vézina supported Balcer's action by rushing the jury and shouting "discrimination" and "your justice is shit."[54] From their Eastern Townships farm, the commune dwellers applauded the courage of these militants and the importance of feminism in the fight for national liberation. We will have to struggle for women's freedom "after the triumph of the revolution, and before it," they insisted.[55]

Life at Petit Québec Libre was an opportunity to rethink traditional roles. There was a lot of work to do on the site: gathering wood, running the sugar shack, repairing the equipment, printing and distributing the commune newspaper, preparing the campground, organizing the daycare activities, setting up workshops, cleaning out the barn before and after every concert, making the meals, washing the dishes, and all the rest. The commune established a rotation of tasks to give the women the equality they were calling for. Surrendering traditional roles was not necessarily an easy thing, though, even if Préfontaine pointed out that "women can do carpentry and men can do the dishes."[56] In fact, the men on kitchen patrol were anything but assiduous. They sabotaged their own work in order to be assigned other responsibilities.[57] The women of the commune had trouble—given their smaller numbers—dislodging men from their traditional roles. There were rarely more than four women in the commune that numbered some twenty members. Charbonneau admitted that this situation caused tension from the very first summer. "We had forgotten to balance out the sex roles," he explained.[58] The commune did not practise "sexual communism"; the underrepresentation of women was felt in the sharing of tasks and decision making.[59]

Préfontaine and Charbonneau did not neglect young people. They promoted Petit Québec Libre on campuses whenever they gave one of their concert forums. The student collective responsible for publishing the paper *Deux mai* was interested enough in what Jazz Libre was doing to reproduce, in its April 1971 issue, the commune's manifesto and a description of the project.[60] It also distributed some of the group's other publications from its offices on Saint-Jean Street in Quebec City. Shunted aside by *Mainmise*, Jazz Libre got some attention in the pages of the magazine thanks to Petit Québec Libre. In the third issue, Jean Basile (writing under the alias Pénélope) proposed a new cartography of an "alternative Quebec." Doc and his bandmates' group did not appear in the "music" category, but the "free jazz farm" was mentioned in the "community life" section.[61] The Sainte-Anne-de-la-Rochelle commune was included as part of "multidimensional Quebec" as conceived of by *Mainmise*.[62] The commune, however, insisted on its links to the left-wing independence movement. It refused "to be a parallel society [...] without any social or political effect," though that did not keep the members from organizing music festivals that appealed to some degree to counterculture youth.[63]

## Schism

The group's political orientation had been on display in Val-David, and it caught the attention of the QPP. Its officers had seized documents and revolutionary recordings as part of the fruitless search for illicit substances at the arts colony. Inevitably, the Sainte-Anne-de-la-Rochelle farm became the object of increased surveillance from the moment the Chénier FLQ cell carried out its actions. The police visited the site five times without making any arrests. Charbonneau, however, nearly met an unfortunate end when he suddenly stepped out of a room holding a trumpet in his hand. The police took the instrument for a weapon but held their fire instead of laying out the musician once and for all.[64] Jazz Libre also had a number of its contracts for concert forums either postponed or cancelled, possibly because of police and government pressure on schools. The group was then arrested on the campus of the Université Laval in Quebec City for passing out copies of the commune's newspaper. Their precarious financial situation and the anxieties of the times kept Préfontaine and Charbonneau constantly on edge.

Petit Québec Libre was the focal point for the police, even before MP Beaudoin's comments in the House of Commons. From an anonymous source, the RCMP received a number of documents picked up at the Maison du Chômeur (a gathering place and resource centre for unemployed workers) in Granby. There were meeting notes, the first issue of the paper *Fête des Travailleurs*, as well as a copy of the commune's manifesto and its publications. The police had already gathered several other issues of *Le P'tit Québec libre*, thanks to informers at the CSN office in Granby and the *Deux mai* newspaper in Quebec City. The QPP was also collecting, on its own, tracts and copies of the commune's publication, as well as accumulating banal details about the supposedly suspicious activities taking place there. Charbonneau and five other individuals, so it was claimed, whiled away a rainy afternoon by planning holdups and kidnappings. This material testified to the militants' actions in the region, at the same time displaying the police surveillance. Among other things, the RCMP was concerned by the fact that the barn at Petit Québec Libre would be able to hold hundreds of people once renovations were finished. The police were worried; they had heard word of an upcoming meeting that would involve American groups such as the Black Panther Party and the Weather Underground.[65]

The RCMP clearly had a reliable source since the meeting did take place at the beginning of September, as scheduled, over the Labour Day weekend. For a week, the commune welcomed members of the Black Panther Party, the Weather Underground, the Young Lords, the Chicanos, and people from Free Vermont and Mayday. More than a hundred militants participated in the activity organized by the Association des Patriotes Vietnamiens de Montréal. This event followed up on the International Day of Solidarity with Political Prisoners that took place in Montreal on August 19, 1970. Several of the groups mentioned were in attendance to promote "active solidarity with revolutionary militants around the world."[66] Petit Québec Libre had its own "international week," which had a similar objective while offering an opportunity for collective reflection on strategies to help overcome capitalism and put an end to imperialist domination.[67] Charbonneau would later state that the commune did not take an active role in the meeting.[68] Yet it certainly did play a role as a facilitator.

To prevent another meeting of the same type between presumed FLQ members and the Black Panthers, four RCMP agents (Claude Brodeur, Bernard Dubuc, Bernard Blier, and Rick Daigle) chose to burn down the commune's barn during the night of May 8 and 9, 1972. The police officers feared a resurgence of violence in Quebec if militant international groups were allowed to help out the so-called wannabe terrorists of the Petit Québec Libre commune. According to the four officers, their intention at the start was to install a listening device in the barn, but technical issues left them no choice other than to turn to arson to force the cancellation of the meeting, or at least a change of venue that would be easier to keep an eye on.

This operation, considered preventative, would be harshly criticized several years later by the Commission d'Enquête sur des Opérations Policières en Territoire Québécois, commonly known as the Keable Commission. This inquiry into police operations in Quebec was set up in 1977 to investigate illegal RCMP actions (theft of dynamite, searches without warrants, dubious recruitment of informers, etc.). The commission concluded that the barn arson was intended, above all, to disrupt Petit Québec Libre's operations and "cause trouble" among commune members.[69] The report raised numerous doubts about the veracity of the stories put forward by RCMP officers. They had not provided sufficient proof of the close links between the Black Panthers and presumed FLQ sympathizers at the commune. They had not shown that they could locate and then put under surveillance the spot where the meeting would have taken place after the arson. They had neglected to explain why they could not count on a human source to document what occurred at the meeting. And to top it off, they had not been able to justify the urgency of such an illegal action considering that they had not intervened at the time of similar past meetings, such as the one in September 1971.[70] Meanwhile, Charbonneau denied that any meeting between militant groups was on the calendar for May 1972.

In a state of consternation, the commune members tried to steady the course during that summer. To raise troop morale and encourage people to visit the commune, they decided to finish off the season with a music festival over the long Labour Day weekend. Préfontaine and Charbonneau took inspiration from their "anti-capitalist festival" in Val-David. French Quebec rock groups Dionysos and O'Cannabis were once again on the bill. Les Champignons, Los Quinchamali, and Les Sinners signed on too.[71] Theatre and film presentations, art workshops, political discussions, and a collective meal around a campfire were also scheduled. Everything was free, and people were asked to contribute according to their means and abilities.

The festival had only just begun, but commune members realized that the counterculture youth who had come for the event were not at all interested by politics. Yet the members had taken the trouble to point out that their project was not aiming for a parallel society or a refuge for drug-taking hippies. "If we're going to fight in a strong and efficient way, we must get rid of the 'sleep rooms' that Quebeckers are using on mass scale. At Petit Québec, we have taken a position against drugs and we urge you to do the same."[72] The message did not get across. The apolitical young people who made the trip out to Sainte-Anne-de-la-Rochelle wanted to get off to the sounds of rock music.

They did not feel like taking the blame for their lack of involvement or being criticized for their consumption of recreational drugs. On the Sunday afternoon, everyone got together to evaluate the experience. The commune members regretted that a number of campers opted to "cave in and zone out" by "getting off" on various substances rather than creating and communicating with their hosts. "As far as the inner revolution is concerned, we're not going to liberate ourselves in Quebec because [. . .] 100,000 people made peace with their inner beings," Préfontaine stated. A camper retorted that Jazz Libre should not have organized a "pop festival" if its intention was really to assemble workers to talk politics.[73] Beckerich was particularly shaken by what he witnessed. "In my little worker's head, I said to myself, if that's the mentality that's leading us, that's our big trip, and the liberation of Quebec is just another trip [. . .], then we're really in for something. Some people are going to take advantage and others are going to get shut out."[74]

Tensions were running high after the end of the festival. During the first year, the commune experimented with collective improvisation. Out of an "anarchistic melting pot," the members established a central council, then created a study committee to find solutions to the problems encountered during the summer of 1971: lack of organization, no connection between personal initiative and common goals, defective internal and external communications due to factionalism, etc.[75] After this self-criticism, they set up a series of committees (administration, finance, activities, coordination, information, external relations, and political action); each was to apply the revolutionary strategies put forward by the central council to their respective fields. Responsible for the activities committee, Jazz Libre was cast into doubt by its counterparts in administration and political action. The band's initiatives were questioned. It was blamed for the disorder of the music festival. We would have opposed the inclusion of rock groups if we had been consulted, they were told. Préfontaine and Charbonneau feared their work would be sabotaged by their colleagues. They even suspected that one of them was an agent provocateur working for the police.

To make matters worse, the expected crowds did not materialize, despite efforts to publicize the commune. The Petit Québec Libre could not find a way to position itself with counterculture youth. Its members also regretted that "the lefty intellectuals have nothing constructive to bring to the project":

> Since the very beginnings of Petit Québec Libre, we've had all sorts of critiques, some good, some bad. [...] It's all well and good to say [...] that the articles in the paper have nothing to say, or that we're too intellectual or not enough or that we swear too much in the paper. [...] Well shit it's great to say what's wrong (most of all it's easy), but it's a lot harder to fix it. We don't think we're the coming of the messiah, and we don't possess the truth. We make mistakes, for sure, but instead of going and telling everyone that this thing and that is fucked at Petit Québec Libre, why not come and help fix it? The more of us there are, the more ideas we'll have. The more ideas we'll have the better things will go.[76]

Whether it was the counterculture youth or the left-wing independence movement, Jazz Libre had its critics on both sides.

Working people as well were resistant to the project. Few families visited the commune during the summer season, except for the long Labour Day weekend. Recruiting participants from the unions was much more difficult than expected, despite the concert forums the group gave in taverns and workers' associations across the province. With the necessary distance, Beckerich would admit that Jazz Libre's music had something to do with their failure. "Already, workers had nothing to do with jazz. And then, when the guys showed up with atonal music, free jazz [...] they had no idea what was going on. They would simply leave." Then he added, "Look, between you and me, I was with the Lapalme guys, and if there hadn't been a strike, if we hadn't had that conflict, I would have been just another guy in the system. I would have been a guy with a good paycheque, a good salary, I would have been happy, and fuck the rest!"[77] Jazz Libre's music action was not only difficult to listen to for the uninitiated, it was generally accompanied by revolutionary speeches that threw people off and repelled some of them, those not already involved in political struggle.

Counterculture youth were not the only ones incredulous when it came to the group's free jazz. Préfontaine and Charbonneau bear some of the blame, since they never questioned their way of working; they were convinced of the social value of collective improvisation in music. This was a surprising failing since self-criticism and listening to others are essential elements in the act of improvising.

They also rejected all structure—which was a drawback when it came to building useful pedagogical approaches, even if their choice fit into their musical practice. This was especially problematic considering that their practice was based on a complex, multidimensional discourse. Yes, the screaming, discordant sound of their music did express a certain kind of revolt. It was also a denial of bourgeois aesthetic conventions and a rebellion against the laws of the marketplace. By definition, their music was anti-capitalist; it was subversive and could not be co-opted. It was also "of the people," since everyone could play it, and it was intended to be inclusive. And that wasn't all. It encouraged communication, participation, and invention through improvisation. In that way, music action offered liberating and bonding experiences through which participants could develop the taste for freedom and the ability to act. Those experiences were then supposed to be transposed into daily life by inventing ways of resisting the capitalist system, then overthrowing it. Yet the group was not just about class conflict. Revolt was an act of taking hold of language—individually and collectively—in an economic order dominated by British and American power. Jazz Libre's music action was there to remind participants that they were both proletariat and colonized, the band's way of referring to the situation of the African diaspora in the United States. Like American free jazz, theirs was a music of decolonization designed to move from individual and collective liberation to national liberation. It was of its time; Quebec's future was to pass through it. At least, that was what Préfontaine and his confreres were attempting to articulate and illustrate. In the end, that was a lot to unpack and assimilate, especially if the primary goal of the audience was to be entertained and have a good time.

***

The RCMP's disruptive tactics were successful; the barn arson exacerbated the latent tensions within Petit Québec Libre. Frustrated in their quest for a true revolutionary praxis, unable to communicate with their audiences, Préfontaine, Charbonneau, and their comrades watched as their utopian project collapsed under the weight of distrust, factionalism, and incomprehension. Police repression and the nature of Jazz Libre's music were not the only reasons for the outcome. The year 1972 was one of transition. The left-wing independence movement was breaking into factions. Some opted for Marxist-Leninist orthodoxy, while others—most notably Pierre Vallières—chose the sovereignty-association approach of the Parti Québécois (PQ), at the time a young political party founded and led by the former Liberal minister René Lévesque. Charbonneau and Préfontaine had to decide which way they would go. They freely interpreted the revolutionary writings they got their hands on and avoided swearing fealty to any one political party. "We are completely Marxists, but not Soviet or Maoist. We believe in a Marxism adapted to North American life and our particular issues."[78] They knew they were at a crossroads—which is why they chose to set up shop in Old Montreal to regroup around their music action and "resolve the contradictions" that compromised their work.[79]

[5]

# The Inevitable Coda
(1973–1975)

*Old Montreal [...] is where "Jazz Libre du Québec" opened the doors of their new club that aims to be something different. Though it's part of a project that follows [...] in the lines of what we know of them from the past.*[1]

–Alain Richardson

On January 27, 1973, Jean Préfontaine sent a letter to the administrators of the Local Initiatives Program (LIP) and reminded them that Jazz Libre needed their support to bring to fruition its "experimental club" project. The group had given dozens of concert forums on a volunteer basis during the previous year thanks to a grant provided by the Ministry of Labour and Immigration. It then decided to use a portion of that funding in mid-September to fix up a space close by Jacques Cartier Square, at 25 Saint Paul Street, in Old Montreal. Designed to be a place of creativity and exchange, L'Amorce ("the beginning," but it can also mean a fuse) would help Jazz Libre concentrate its energies on the creation and democratization of an innovative people's culture while bringing in new individuals into its network. Building a common front of cultural workers "responds to an urgent need felt in Montreal circles for an organization of cultural exploration which, instead of being cut off from the population [...], will try to involve it through activities and participation," Préfontaine explained to LIP management.[2] To no avail: it would not reverse its decision to suspend financing of the project, forcing Jazz Libre to invest all its savings into L'Amorce so the group could continue its activities beyond Petit Québec Libre.

Moving to Montreal a few weeks after Labour Day 1972 was no accident. Préfontaine and Yves Charbonneau were exhausted by the commune's internal strife and frustrated in their desire to extend the reach of their cultural activities. The two men had no choice other than to leave Sainte-Anne-de-la-Rochelle to refocus on their music action. L'Amorce was their constructive response to the failure of their project of shaping a common front of opposition movements. With this experimental culture venue, the two musicians hoped to break with sectarian political militancy and get themselves out of police surveillance. They still believed in the mobilizing potential of their music; for them, it remained a true anti-imperialist and anti-capitalist praxis. Yet they were having trouble positioning Jazz Libre among the schisms that were rocking the leftist independence movement at the beginning of 1972. As we will see in this last chapter, those schisms would leave their mark on the group as it strove to redefine itself and find a "common thread of action."[3] Those fault lines would make it impossible to breathe new life into Jazz Libre after the arson that would destroy L'Amorce in 1974.

## Local Initiatives

It was surprising that a program created in 1971 by the Trudeau government—the same administration that dusted off the War Measures Act and suggested to the Lapalme guys to "go eat shit"—would be used to finance the operations of musicians known for their revolutionary ideas.[4] The LIP's mandate was to fight unemployment by giving grants for short-term projects that would help jobless people. At the beginning of the 1970s, with Quebec's unemployment rate at 7.3% and unions at the top of their game, the program was very popular. The RCMP knew about Préfontaine, and logically, his request for a grant for cultural activism would have been refused. But the committees that evaluated the requests were made up of people in the communities involved in the particular fields, at least during the first year, and they operated independently of the police. Jazz Libre was evidently not concerned with the paradox of money from Ottawa being used to broadcast its seditious music and finance its socialist commune.

With the amounts they received through the LIP, Préfontaine and Charbonneau were able to hire new musicians, minimizing the personnel turnover that had plagued Jazz Libre ever since it left L'Infonie and set up shop in Sainte-Anne-de-la-Rochelle. Tristan Honsinger was among those who came on board during that period. Born in 1949 in Burlington, Vermont, Honsinger trained as a classical cellist before heading to Canada in 1969 to resist the Vietnam draft. He first travelled to Quebec City but in the end chose Montreal, where he discovered he had talent as an improviser. His work followed along the same lines as that of European musicians such as Evan Parker and Derek Bailey, whose improvisation was non-idiomatic—that is, not tied to any specific musical language. The experimental approach Honsinger was working on in the fall of 1971 had nothing to do with classical music anymore; nor did it have any attachment to avant-garde jazz. All the same, Préfontaine and Charbonneau could hear a connection between their music and the free improvisations of the young musician standing before them, alone, cello in hand, in an alley that gave onto Jacques Cartier Square. Blown away by what they heard, they asked Honsinger to join their group for a series of concert forums set for the next year.

Percussionist Jean-Guy Poirier also joined Jazz Libre at the beginning of 1972. Born in 1937 in Saint-Alexandre-des-Lacs in the Lower Saint Lawrence region, he had been living in Montreal since the start of the 1950s. His idea, when he reached the city, was to become a trumpet player, but his search for a cheap instrument, by a strange set of circumstances, ended up with him buying a drum kit. Poirier quickly picked up a multifaceted musical education which had him accompanying various bands in Montreal and elsewhere in the province. He met Charbonneau for the first time on the cabaret circuit at the beginning of the 1960s. At the time, both were interested in new forms of jazz without necessarily being ready to completely throw themselves into experimentation. They lost track of each other for several years until, one day, Charbonneau came across Poirier in Saint-Louis Square, banging on a set of bongos and conga drums. The meeting was fortuitous: Jazz Libre had been searching for a full-time drummer ever since Cyril Lepage and Curly Virgil's short stints with the group in Val-David. Poirier agreed to join the band on one condition: they lend him the money to buy a new drum kit. He would stay with the group until autumn 1973, with a ten-month break when Patrice Beckerich would step in, from summer 1972 until spring of the following year.

The money provided by the LIP grant also allowed Jazz Libre to officially hire bassist Jean Martineau. Born in Montreal in 1947, he had been helping out the group from time to time. He was a jazzophile, as well as being a fixture on the Montreal rock scene, and went from electric bass to guitar during his adventure with free jazz that lasted several months. Jacques Beaudoin replaced him at the end of spring 1972. Beaudoin was born in the Beauce region south of Quebec City in 1950 and was enamoured with psychedelic rock until he discovered the upright bass. He felt compelled to experiment with the instrument after hearing a remarkable *Jazz en liberté* concert on the airwaves of Radio-Canada in May 1969. The concert featured bassist Michel Donato with Brian Barley on sax, Claude Ranger on drums, and Alan Penfold on trumpet. Then and there, Beaudoin made the decision to study music. He joined L'Infonie shortly after the group's break with Jazz Libre, to improve his playing both on stage and in the studio. Walter Boudreau was the one to mention that Préfontaine and his bandmates were looking for a bass player. Beaudoin's sojourn with Jazz Libre was of short duration, since he returned to L'Infonie in the summer of 1972.

Next it was Yves Bouliane's turn to take the stage. Born in Montreal in 1952, he studied classical bass with Roland Desjardins at the Montreal Conservatory at the beginning of the 1970s. He was not even twenty when he started improvising with a trio that included Robert M. Lepage (clarinet) and Roger Boudreau (guitar). He discovered Jazz Libre on the third floor of the Association Espagnole one summer evening in 1969. The group was a quintet at the time: Préfontaine and Charbonneau with Guy Thouin, Jacques Valois, and Gaby Johnston. They were standing, tightly grouped "like soldiers" in a room that was all but empty, playing with "vehemence" and "total physical discipline."[5] Bouliane was dumbstruck by what he saw and heard: the musicians' integrity, their rebellious nature, and their total involvement in the act of collective creation that produced a pure, authentic sound. The experience was obviously formative. It fed his explorations and placed him unexpectedly on Jazz Libre's path at the beginning of autumn 1972.

Bouliane discovered a different group that year—expanded and ready to find new audiences thanks to LIP grant financing. With the title "LE JAZZ LIBRE DU QUÉBEC," Initiative #211-2437 lasted ten months (February 1 to November 30, 1972) on an $85,000 budget. Some forty people, twenty-seven men and thirteen women, worked on the tour, visiting "culturally disadvantaged areas" like the Pointe-Saint-Charles district of Montreal.[6] These presentations were meant to help "democratize accessibility to culture," encourage "active participation from the public," promote "music as a means of communication," and move people to "organize to practice collective improvisation and so creatively fill their leisure time."[7] The group used the opportunity to conduct a survey into the cultural habits of its different audiences. "It isn't federal espionage," Préfontaine insisted.[8] He and his bandmates looked into the number of hours audience members spent in front of their TV sets, the kinds of shows they were watching, the number of live concerts they could afford per year, and their preferences when it came to a stage play, a classical music performance, a popular music presentation, a movie, or a hockey game.[9] The survey and the LIP grant it was attached to were similar to the cultural projects that Jazz Libre had been undertaking since 1968.

The LIP financing made it possible for Jazz Libre to team up with painter and artist Pierre Monat to make a video of the group's concert forums. Called *Y'a du dehors dedans* ("there's outside inside"), the document features an experimental soundtrack, jumpy editing, compelling interviews, and a series of video feedback. It is an amazing work somewhere between documentary and experimental art. Monat was not looking for a visual equivalent for Jazz Libre's music. He was not trying to illustrate it through his own improvisation. He called his approach "situationist" in the sense that he was interested in the way the musicians occupied space and the ways they entered into contact with each other and with their audiences. Monat stated, "To act by taking action, creating situations, contexts, acting in context, that's what moved the guys [...] to become political militants." By not making a didactic video, he was able to participate in the music, whether it was "illustratable" or not.[10]

The influx of new participants led to greater energy. The screening of *Y'a du dehors dedans* was an opportunity for some self-examination. The video was shown at the Vidéographe coop, as the first part of a concert forum, for a week in early February 1973. Charbonneau and Préfontaine reflected out loud on the origins of the group, its political orientation, tumultuous history, and the evolution of its music. Suddenly a voice spoke up. A young man in the room wanted to know the difference between Jazz Libre making improvised sounds and everyday noise. Bouliane answered by relating an experience of deep listening to street recordings, such as the sound of cars or pedestrians' footsteps. He explained, "Music is everywhere. You don't hear it all the time, but sometimes you can grasp it. Then you get a moment that is beautiful, poetic, musical, that is [...] complete in itself." Préfontaine went on to give his version of things, differentiating street noise from what musicians do. Their music action was not just random, since the results of their improvisation translated the players' "mental structures." Charbonneau added that people should not "hear it only as sounds and noises," since the political activism of the group "brought it to other places than just playing sounds."[11] These three answers, all distinct, reflected the group's efforts to rethink the borders of their music.

## A New Beginning

Their evolution and return to Montreal heralded a change of orientation for the 1973 summer season. The previous summer had been particularly difficult for Petit Québec Libre. It had begun with the arson of the barn and ended with the disorder of the Labour Day weekend. Préfontaine and Charbonneau needed a change; they were discouraged, even disillusioned, by what they saw at the dozens of concert forums they gave as part of their LIP activities. The two musicians were tired of explaining the theoretical foundation of their music to audiences "who were always changing and not necessarily interested."[12] They had run out of words trying to answer those who judged that Jazz Libre did "anything whenever they felt like it" with their instruments. Préfontaine no longer hoped to convert young people to free jazz, while Charbonneau was disappointed by the workers' lack of participation. He was often told, "Shut your trap and just play."[13] The group provided their audiences with percussion instruments to introduce them to collective improvisation, but some of them, under the influence of alcohol, damaged the drums by beating on them with beer bottles. Such events convinced Jazz Libre to break off its tour and look for a permanent place to play in the city. It hoped to develop a loyal and involved audience willing to come to them in their chosen spot. "A long time ago, we understood that it takes several concerts for some people to appreciate our music, and since it's new and modern, less open-minded audiences have trouble with it at first," Préfontaine explained.[14]

Setting up an experimental culture centre seemed to be the answer to the band's urgent need to regroup and rethink its music—a new beginning to build a new network of people to work with. They began their move into L'Amorce in mid-September 1972, digging into their LIP grant money. The funds would run out at the end of November, but Préfontaine was sure that the financing would be recurrent, since the committee whose job it was to evaluate ongoing projects had approved this change of direction. A few months later, Jazz Libre was surprised to learn that its project was "suspended," since it was now considered "not a priority."[15] This turnaround was probably the result of the closer relations the RCMP was developing with LIP administrators. Whatever the reason, the group had no choice other than to finance itself if it wanted to bring its new project to term.

L'Amorce opened its doors officially in August 1973, though Jazz Libre had been playing there since the previous autumn. The experimental venue was located on the ground floor of a three-storey building administered by the Association Coopérative Ouvrière de Production—les Amis du Québec (the ACOPAQ, or, roughly, "the workers' cooperative production association"). The organization was the idea of the Dead Men's Club, a bikers' group from the Saint-Henri neighbourhood, facilitated by social worker Gisèle Désormeaux. The ACOPAQ acquired the building at 21-25 Saint-Paul Street in July 1972, once again thanks to an LIP grant. On the second floor, members of the Dead Men's Club made toys (giant abacuses, wooden ducks, model boats, and building blocks) as part of a rehabilitation project. The third floor was occupied by Monat and his Pathografik colleagues. The Jardin des glaces, an ice-cream shop where jazzmen and folk singers sometimes played, stood at street level just west of the building. The Patapalace—the name given to this unusual collection—faced the Black Bottom, a nightclub patronized by the city's jazzophiles. A few steps from there, on Jacques Cartier Square, were a number of cabarets where music lovers of all kinds converged on the weekends. After two years in the countryside, Jazz Libre had gone all in when it came to the Montreal cultural scene.

Though it seemed like a fresh start, L'Amorce was intended to be a continuation of the cultural action that Jazz Libre had begun at the end of the 1960s, then developed in Val-David and Sainte-Anne-de-la-Rochelle.

The difficulties at Petit Québec Libre led the group to concentrate its energies exclusively on the cultural aspect of the leftist independence movement. For Charbonneau, this kind of repositioning necessarily brought with it a collective self-criticism in order to "resolve the contradictions within Jazz Libre du Québec." He believed the members of the group had to commit to supporting each other and adopt a common political stance. Which was why L'Amorce needed to function along the lines of "democratic centralism" while promoting mutual help, communication, equality, and self-discipline.[16] These goals aligned with the objectives listed in the LIP grant proposal, except that everyone—members of Jazz Libre and those they worked with—was also expected to adopt a resolutely revolutionary attitude. "We are working on the exploration, experimentation, and presentation of a new Quebec culture, anti-capitalist and of the people, while ridding ourselves of the boss-employee contradiction [...], where musicians and artists act like trained monkeys," as Charbonneau put it.[17]

The way the space worked at L'Amorce served the new people's culture. First, there was no stage at 25 Saint-Paul Street. The musicians played among the audience and urged them to participate and enter the performance. Placing speakers in the four corners of the room helped them reconfigure the audience–performer relationship. Alain Richardson, journalist at *Pop jeunesse*, was pleasantly surprised by the arrangement that he described as a way of "knocking down the myth of the show with its superheroes and the walls that separate them from those of us listening."[18] Even back at Petit Québec Libre, the group fought "against the artist star system built on the back of big bucks, and against so-called popular forms of escapist music."[19] L'Amorce continued in that direction by asking people to take part in jazz-infused experiences conceived "outside of the commercial criteria of petty bourgeois culture."[20]

By refocusing on its music action, Jazz Libre hoped to redefine the role it would play in remaking Quebec society. To do so, the group needed to clearly set down the theories of its foundation. The tracts the band handed out took up some of the ideas put forward by Patrick Straram in *Parti pris*. Among them: jazz is an "art of protest" and a refusal "to escape this world," necessarily leading to collective awareness, and the vector of a true people's culture since it is part of social structures.[21] But the group did not limit itself to this idiom in its efforts to renew its revolutionary practice. It had already made it clear that its collective improvisation, though inspired by African American free jazz, was necessarily rooted in the French-speaking and European heritage of the group's members. Jazz Libre was becoming increasingly interested in experimental work found in some contemporary music (such as serialism, concrete music, and minimalism), even if such styles were not normally thought of as soundtracks for struggles against imperialism and capitalism. The members of the group saw no contradiction. "If our anger is our only energy left, then we have to use it esthetically. It has to become form and technique as well as the content of our expression. There's no other way."[22]

L'Amorce would be a meeting place for creative cultural workers of all stripes and disciplines. Like the Technique d'Action Sociale unit of the Fusion des Arts group, Jazz Libre intended to use the mobilizing capacities of different art forms (music, dance, theatre, poetry, video, etc.) to bring new dynamism to politico-cultural activism in Quebec. Its experimental culture centre, self-governed and non-profit, was just the place for that. Préfontaine and Charbonneau were hoping to meet up again with Serge Lemoyne, Lucie Barash, Raôul Duguay, and the Théâtre des Travailleurs. They were also considering collaborations with theatre directors Jean-Pierre Ronfard and Claude Couillard, as well as with the dancers from the Groupe de la Place Royale. Meanwhile, Honsinger founded a free improvisational trio with clarinetist Peter Bastiaan and choreographer Hélène Filion. L'Amorce was also receptive to the new generation of improvisers (Jean Derome, Robert Leriche, Bryan Highbloom, and Michel-Georges Brégent, to name a few) who were opening up fresh musical pathways.

Jazz Libre was building its common front of cultural workers in two ways. First, the group renewed its network by providing a place where creation and exchange could happen. Then it enlarged the network by taking part in the founding of Relève-Kébek, a parallel circuit of creative centres that covered most of the province, from Dorion just off the island of Montreal to Mont-Laurier in the upper Laurentians, and Montreal and Quebec City. L'Amorce, La Grande Passe, La Casanous, and the Trois Points Virgule were among the Montreal venues that functioned "outside the system." They opposed the co-opting of "alternative culture" and the "world of the underground."[23] You could see anything on their stages: music, movies, theatre, dance, lectures, as well as visual art shows. It cost $1 to enter, and the content was exclusively made in Quebec. Like L'Amorce, Trois Points Virgule (on Bloomfield Avenue) enjoyed LIP grant funding, while La Grande Passe (on Ontario Street) was managed by a cooperative made up of some twenty members. La Casanous, the oldest of the four, was a private company established in 1971 on the third floor of the Association Espagnole, where Jazz Libre ended up after its employment at The Barrel was terminated in winter of 1968. The group did return to play there several times during the months leading up to the opening of L'Amorce.

## Disunity

These new orientations were developing against a background of profound changes on the Quebec left. The events of October 1970 and the resulting police repression led opposition movements to reconsider their strategies. The arrival of the Parti Québécois (PQ) on the political scene changed the game, the same way the inter-union mobilization had occurred, followed by the arrest of three prominent union leaders. The opposite paths taken by FLQ members Charles Gagnon and Pierre Vallières illustrated the split in the leftist independence movement at the time. Basing himself in part on the work of the Comités d'Action Politique in the Montreal districts of Saint-Jacques and Maisonneuve, Gagnon believed that Quebec should prioritize the political organization of the proletariat along Marxist lines. According to him, the socialist revolution would come about by the proletariat taking power; he then went on to found the Marxist-Leninist group En Lutte![24] Meanwhile, Vallières was exhorting his comrades to support the PQ:

> In some so-called "advanced" sectors of the Quebec left, the *a priori* refusal to give any form of *real* support to the Parti Québécois, in the present situation, is the result of a truncated analysis of the national question in Quebec and not [...] "Marxist-Leninist" revolutionary thinking. Some leftists want to skip the national issue. They even hope that the PQ will never take power, believing that in the current colonial structures, the workers will develop revolutionary class consciousness and opt for independence when they feel they can give that status a completely socialist content. But to think that is to forget that in a colonialized society, the independence of a nation is not just one issue among many for workers—it's the *most important issue.*[25]

The polarization of the leftist independence movement complicated Jazz Libre's efforts to redefine itself.

And that was all the truer at that point, since the group had stopped reaching out to workers as it did in the days of the commune and the concert forums held under the auspices of LIP grants. Jazz Libre was in no position to take the pulse of the situation in working-class districts since it had chosen to retreat back to its music. It also missed the chance to encounter new groups of young people inspired by the Maoist Marxist-Leninist theories that were spreading across Montreal campuses, in particular the ideas that led to the founding of the Mouvement Révolutionnaire Étudiant du Québec ("student revolutionary movement") in 1972. This organization focused its energies on political action in institutions of learning and working-class milieus with an emphasis on internationalist thinking—which included the Association des Patriotes Vietnamiens de Montréal, a group that Jazz Libre had supported in 1971 during the "international week" at Petit Québec Libre. Préfontaine and his colleagues inevitably found themselves distanced from the places where militants were active, now that they had decided to set themselves up at L'Amorce.

Jazz Libre would be there nonetheless when the time came to make a favourable impression on Italian Communist Party (PCI) sympathizers. The group made the acquaintance of Italian composer Albert Mayr who, in 1970, received a grant from the Canada Council in electronic music and later became a lecturer at the McGill Faculty of Music in 1973. Mayr discovered L'Amorce somewhat by accident on an outing with students in Old Montreal. He heard Jazz Libre there, got friendly with the musicians, and gave a recording of one of their performances to the artistic director of the Autunno Musicale festival, an annual avant-garde event on the shores of Lake Como. Shortly afterward, Jazz Libre received an invitation. Outside of the dates with Robert Charlebois in Ontario and France, the group had never played its music beyond Quebec. Bouliane had left them a month earlier, so Richard would be going on the trip to the Italian Alps with Préfontaine, Charbonneau, and Poirier.

Jazz Libre's performance at the festival would have been satisfactory, and no more, if it hadn't been for its jazz interpretation of "The Internationale." For the past several years, the group finished its performances with an improvisation on the theme of the revolutionary hymn composed in 1871 by Eugène Pottier, a member of the Paris Commune. "We play and sing THE INTERNATIONALE because we believe in it, and because it is truly international, just like music, like any act of liberation. We believe there are two cultures the way there are two classes: the exploiters have theirs, and we have ours," Charbonneau declared.[26] Sung around the world by people in left-wing movements of all kinds, the revolutionary hymn, just like free jazz, was for the trumpetist and his bandmates the universal soundtrack of the struggle of the oppressed classes. The piece was necessarily part of their repertoire when they got off the plane in Italy.

Jazz Libre came on stage at the Villa Olmo early in the evening of September 30, 1973. Poirier caught his bandmates off guard by sitting down behind a set of timbales left on the edge of the stage for another performance scheduled later that evening. The group's first piece went on for quite some time; scattered here and there were ominous drum rolls and strident horn attacks. Then Poirier moved to centre stage and sat down behind his drum kit and suddenly struck up a military march on his snare. The horns immediately joined him and burst out with the theme from "The Internationale." The audience was completely surprised. The year before, the PCI had maintained its position as the official opposition in parliament. Poirier would remember the audience getting to its feet after a few seconds of the theme; Communist Party sympathizers interpreted it as a sincere expression of support from these musicians from Canada.[27] Jazz Libre had not planned to stay on past the Lake Como date, but their Villa Olmo performance earned them two further invitations, October 15 and 16, at Milan's Teatro Uomo. "Power to the imagination, power to the people," read the poster promoting Jazz Libre's "socialist adventure."[28] It did not lead to international fame, but the enthusiastic response of the Italian left did stimulate the group.

But Jazz Libre could not maintain the momentum when it returned home because of further personnel turnover. An altercation between Charbonneau and Poirier in Italy (the two were apparently courting the same woman, and alcohol entered the equation) forced the group to go looking for a new drummer in the fall. Richard recruited Mathieu Léger. Born in the Ottawa suburbs in 1952, he studied classical percussion before moving into progressive rock and hitting the stage at Manseau's Woodstock Pop Festival as part of the band Lasting Weep. Léger was exploring other types of music when he ran into Richard in a Montreal bar. His joining the group coincided with it moving toward new musical fields. The hard-hitting, strident free jazz of the beginning years was slowly giving way to long pieces based on calmer atmospheres, silences, and a desire to design sound spaces from improvised gestures both discreet and immersive. The move came at a good time; the group was set to record the soundtrack of a documentary on the work of an old friend of Préfontaine's, poet Claude Gauvreau, who died in tragic circumstances on July 7, 1971.

The soundtrack of *Claude Gauvreau—Poète* (Jean-Claude Labrecque, 1974) reflects Jazz Libre's musical influences since they settled in at L'Amorce. The group was moving progressively from free jazz toward other experimental practices characterized by innovative compositional forms, the search for new sounds, including silences, and a more diverse instrumentation. "More and more we are leaving […] wild protest for a more inner music that mixes free jazz with what is happening in contemporary music," Préfontaine explained to journalist and writer Gilles Archambault.[29] Doc was finally ready to move in the direction suggested by Thouin at the beginning of the 1970s. The group's former drummer had insisted on the need to use "silence as much as notes" and to explore contemporary music to move the band forward.[30] Now Préfontaine was beginning to rethink his music action in aesthetic and introspective terms.

Charbonneau was not so sure that such a move was relevant, though he, too, was interested in the experimental forms of contemporary music. He found that the audience response was unconvincing in many cases. "Who are those people who think we're funny when we play soft, when we play at the level of notes. And who are the people who like us when we're aggressive?" Strident, dissonant improvisations "express a Quebec reality," he maintained. It was all about class struggle, and that was why the bourgeoisie "gets the hell out" when the music turns stormy and intense.[31] Charbonneau believed that the work had to stay political, since new Quebec culture would come into being only through a process of liberation. It is safe to say that he regretted Jazz Libre's decision to retreat into creation and cultural animation rather than venturing further into agitprop.

The discord between Préfontaine and Charbonneau reflected their political differences. The latter was leaning quite clearly toward Marxist-Leninist thought without completely submitting to the idea that the proletariat cause held sway over the nationalist one. He, too, suffered from the same disarray that afflicted the leftist independence movement after the October Crisis. Intransigent, though dismayed by the fact that the group could not get its message across, he exhorted his colleagues not to let up, and stay in the fight. Meanwhile, Préfontaine adopted a more nuanced way of thinking that would presumably allow Jazz Libre to adjust to the tenor of the times. Instead of following the Marxist-Leninist line, the group needed to take it upon itself to "push the PQ more to the left, toward social democracy, to avoid the totalitarianism and fascism that comes with national socialism."[32] Préfontaine had less and less patience for Charbonneau's extremist declarations, while the latter was increasingly exasperated by his colleague's bourgeois attitude. Needless to say, the idea of a common political stance now seemed impossible, especially since the two no longer appeared able to communicate effectively.

The tense atmosphere left its mark on Jazz Libre over the months before and after the trip to Italy. Léger would remember that the two men often argued and that they had a way of playing against each other. One time out of three, that pattern resulted in quality collective improvisations, especially when the rhythm section joined in.[33] Bouliane would add that, on both sides, they were totally dedicated to Jazz Libre's projects when it was necessary.[34] Monat would agree with these observations; the group's strength arose from this dichotomy:

> Jazz Libre was Préfontaine and Charbonneau. Charbonneau was the proletariat. Préfontaine was petty bourgeois. Préfontaine had an "education"—

> don't forget the quotation marks. He was very closed off in a certain way. Which led him to be messianic when it came to his music. [...] Charbonneau, on the other hand, was more or less a cultural Bolshevik who had no academic background in the traditional sense. [...] You always felt that Préfontaine had a whole set of references. And all those references, as a rule, could be heavy to carry. While Charbonneau played by instinct, instinctive in the sense that he was self-governing in a way that Préfontaine couldn't be; Préfontaine could be more institutional. The conflicts, depending on the number of beers they drank, broke out along those fault lines. But Jazz Libre could have never existed without that dialectic.[35]

Up to a certain point, those tensions were constructive, and they even made for fertile ground for the music and the organization. But that would not be enough when the time came to face the test of another disastrous fire.

The night of June 24 and 25 saw the event that propelled Jazz Libre toward its dissolution. That evening, more than 10,000 Montrealers converged on Jacques Cartier Square to celebrate Saint-Jean-Baptiste Day. Disruptive behaviour on the part of the partygoers had the police intervening. The situation quickly turned into a riot, fires were lit, and in the uproar, flames were seen leaping from the building that housed L'Amorce. The firefighters had trouble reaching the heart of Old Montreal because of the disorder in the streets. When they finally made it to the spot, it took them three hours to tame the blaze. The Jazz Libre musicians were able to save part of the equipment, but it was too little too late. The inspectors sent to 21-25 Saint-Paul Street found gas cans in each of the two elevator shafts. The city's fire service concluded it was a case of arson.[36] But the police inquiry would never find the guilty parties.[37]

The members of Jazz Libre believed that the fire was set by the same person who presumably helped those who burned down the barn at Petit Québec Libre. According to what Charbonneau remembered, someone at the commune passed out beer to everyone to get them drunk so they would fall into a deep sleep a few hours before the barn caught fire.[38] The same individual was allegedly spotted near L'Amorce the evening of Saint-Jean-Baptiste Day 1974. The police apparently tried unsuccessfully to find him, then closed the inquiry.[39] Charbonneau and his colleagues suspected he was either a pyromaniac, or a deranged person with a personal vendetta against the group, or, worse, an agent provocateur working for the RCMP. The latter theory gained ground in the fall of 1977 with the revelations of the Keable Commission. Charbonneau tried to throw light on the story by confiding his suspicions to journalist Steve Kowch. Those working for the commission would briefly get interested in the articles in *The Gazette*, though they never tried to establish a link between the burning of the barn and the fire at L'Amorce. No one would ever be accused in the second case of arson.

***

That event was the beginning of the end for Jazz Libre. Discouraged and unable to resolve his differences with

Charbonneau, Préfontaine left his bandmates the day after the fire. The rest of the group moved its headquarters and what was left of its instruments first to La Grande Passe, then to the Centre d'Essai le Conventum, on Sanguinet Street, where it hoped to recover. The fertile discord between Charbonneau and Préfontaine would never be equalled, though Jazz Libre found enough strength in its music action to carry on a few more months. The closing concert at the Rencontre Internationale de la Contre-Culture on Sunday, April 27, 1975, was the group's last chance to get its message across and excoriate the establishment. Michel Madore, Serge Vaillancourt, Normand Cataford, Philippe Gingras (alias Baron Filip), and several other artists joined Jazz Lib' du Kebek (the spelling chosen for the event) in a festive atmosphere that culminated—no surprise there—with a collective improvisation on a theme often visited by Charbonneau and his colleagues. It was "The Internationale," the symbol of a new era that, though Jazz Libre would never see it, seemed at the time to be near at hand.[30]

# Conclusion

In 1989, the Montreal International Jazz Festival intended to celebrate its tenth anniversary with a special program featuring Jazz Libre. The band that was to take the stage at the Université du Québec à Montréal on Saturday, July 8, was the same that had recorded for London Records of Canada and Radio-Canada International in 1968: the founding members of the group accompanied by pianist Pierre Nadeau. Jean Préfontaine, Maurice Richard, and Yves Charbonneau were obviously not in top form since they had stopped playing music professionally after the band broke up in 1975. Guy Thouin had returned to jazz after a long hiatus due to an extended stay in India. Yet everyone was expecting a concert for the history books:

> Jazz Libre du Québec was an eye witness to an all-important chapter in Quebec history. The end of the sixties, a turbulent time when culture, just like the province itself, had definitely asserted its quest for identity. One of the rare bands to play free jazz, Jazz Libre was the central core that formed L'Infonie, as well as accompanying Robert Charlebois during his meteoric rise. A show that no one was expecting, since the group broke up some fifteen years ago.[1]

As the festival date approached, the five musicians were rehearsing with great conviction at Thouin's place. The atmosphere recalled the proto-commune on Papineau Street, where they had laid down the foundations of their music action.

But their disappointment was total. Not because of a lukewarm performance but because the concert was cancelled. Apparently, not enough tickets were sold. The loss of the radio broadcasting partner and a poor promotion campaign were also to blame.[2] Were people afraid that Jazz Libre would not be up to the task after years of inactivity? Or did someone have regrets about inviting left-wing "musical terrorists" to a festival that was a big part of the cultural industries that Montreal depended on to attract summertime tourists? Whatever the case, Jazz Libre was not at home in the festival. The group's music action had certainly lost some of its vitality and urgency. Its theoretical foundations were out of date in the Quebec of the 1980s, and the politically engaged, active listening on which it depended was also a thing of the past. All the same, the band's music was and would remain—in its form and its content, as well as in its refusal to be reduced to entertainment with no social meaning—an example of sound resistance in Quebec's cultural landscape.

This latest setback hit the group hard. It was part of the political climate that recalled the failure of the leftist nationalist project in which the band members had invested everything between 1967 and 1975. Hopes were high when the PQ came to power in 1976, which made the defeat of the "Yes" side in the 1980 referendum on sovereignty association all the more painful. The return of Robert Bourassa's Liberals to power—the same Bourassa who reigned over the October Crisis and opened the door to the police repression of the left—was certainly no cause for celebration, even if the Liberals did try to promote the idea that Quebec was a "distinct society" within Canadian federalism. At the beginning of the 1990s, American hegemony widened its influence as Canada entered a new period of neoliberalism by signing the North American Free Trade Agreement (NAFTA). Marxist-Leninist militants were ineffectual; they had been adrift since the En lutte! group dissolved, and after the Communist Workers Party did the same earlier in the decade. At the end of the 1980s, expectations gave way to incomprehension, bitterness, and disillusionment. It did not look like there would be a Jazz Libre reunion or a return to the project of an independent, French-speaking, socialist Quebec. The province's status as a "distinct society" would not be recognized either.

For eight years, Charbonneau, Préfontaine, and their many colleagues (some more ambivalent than others), as well as the left-wing independence movement that inspired them, situated their project of a French-speaking, socialist, independent Quebec within the international context of decolonization. They developed their revolutionary thinking and articulated their music action, finding inspiration in writings (*The Little Red Book*, newspapers like *Sud Vietnam en lutte* and *The Guardian*) and cultural production (American free jazz) that were international in scope. Their search for a revolutionary practice involved the appropriation of an African American music that could support the discourse of the times about the political, economic, and cultural exploitation of the colonized French Canadians who were the subject of Pierre Vallières's book. Jazz Libre wanted its music to be inclusive, an invitation to mobilize. All their initiatives (the concert forums, the Val-David arts colony, Petit Québec Libre, and L'Amorce) were based on this idea; they were experiments in communication, organization, and participation. Theirs was "a happy and aggressive cry of freedom, a cry of relief, a bursting forward of life, a bold and healthy affirmation."[3] It was, in the final analysis, "an art of protest."[4]

Yet the uninitiated heard only noise and saw no structuring principle, despite the efforts expended to convince them that collective improvisation really was the music of the people. Which is why the working class did not answer the band's call. The common front created at Petit Québec Libre was the opportunity to ally radical feminists with left-wing nationalists, but there were very few women at the commune, and Jazz Libre remained an all-male band, a consequence of the underrepresentation of women both in the Montreal jazz scene and among leftist separatists. Despite its appropriation of free jazz and appeal to decolonization, Jazz Libre followed the example of the *Parti pris* group by neglecting the city's different ethnic communities that made it a crossroads for more than one diaspora. The same was true for the First Nations, despite the fact that they were directly concerned with the band's nationalism, and that improvisation was—and still is—at the heart of their musical traditions.

Jazz Libre's music was out of touch with the political and cultural reality of working families and was largely deaf to the demands of minorities left behind by the left-wing independence movement. It was also challenged from within (*a posteriori*, in most cases) by musicians who were not convinced by the leftist rhetoric of Charbonneau and Préfontaine. Patrice Beckerich maintained that free jazz was too hard to listen to for people who lacked the tools to decipher it. Yves Bouliane said more or less the same thing. Jazz Libre's collective improvisations were so much cacophony for the uninitiated, even if the music was the product of a complete and admirable "effort of construction." Mathieu Léger felt the same way. For him, the words used by Charbonneau and Préfontaine to explain free jazz to working people were "completely disconnected from reality." He stated categorically that "this music was not of the people." Jacques Beaudoin added, "The working class doesn't get off on it." Jean-Guy Poirier went further in his critique. He believed that the group's insistence on playing "The Internationale" and larding every performance with political speeches were mistakes, since the band closed itself off from the contemporary music scene that it could have expanded into. Its music action was wholly linked to the fate of the left-wing independence movement of the 1970s. Thouin did concede that his confreres were true to themselves. "You know, they said free, everyone had to be free, and Quebec had to be free, too."[5]

Jazz Libre's dilemma had deep foundations. The group's travails arose from the problem of transposing a certain type of American postwar music, which emerged from certain social structures, onto Quebec. In the process, Jazz Libre exposed the limits of the metaphors deployed to legitimize leftist nationalism in the province and underscored the challenges attendant on renewing and democratizing popular culture—in other words, the limits to the very notion of praxis and the possibility of reconciling theory and practice. Still, the group was a perfect example of the important role played by cultural workers in the resistance movements in Quebec. In that way, it incarnated a critical voice that kept up its opposition to the powers in place.

As well, Jazz Libre inspired a younger generation of improvisers who, though less inclined to let identity politics dictate how they worked, continued on the path taken by their predecessors, turning Quebec into a hot spot of improvised music. Among them, we can cite Bouliane, Robert M. Lepage, Michel Di Torre, and Raymond Gervais, co-founders of the Atelier de Musique Expérimentale (AME) in 1973. Others rapidly joined them (to name a few, Vincent Dionne, Bernard Gagnon, and Bryan Highbloom) and helped build a community of improvisers, giving them the space and tools necessary to self-produce and assert their voices. Most of these musicians were born between 1945 and 1955, and their teenage years were formed by the counterculture and the fallout from FLQ terrorism in a Quebec that was counting on young people for the future. They were less apt to opt for their predecessors' revolutionary leftist ideas. Still, they sought inspiration in Jazz Libre's work to democratize music and establish networks—self-governing, independent, possessing their own spaces—outside of official culture. They listened, decoded, and worked out collective improvisation on their own terms. By listening to free jazz, yes, but also to other forms of experimental music. They were trying to push their understanding of the creative acts through which individuals situate themselves in the world, while expanding their inventory of sound-making materials that could be integrated into their spontaneous and sometimes playful creations, alone or in a group, using both professional and amateur musicians, on stage or in daily life.

The AME broke up in 1975 and was not in a position to ensure the survival of improvised music in Quebec's cultural landscape at the end of the 1970s. The nationalist fervour that brought the PQ to power generated a renewed interest in French-language folklore. Rock music sung in French had a role to play as well, but the new improvised music, instrumental in most cases, was suspect. "Left on the sidelines," the new generation of improvisers got busy organizing.[6] In 1977, Robert Leriche, Claude Simard, Pierre Saint-Jacques, and Jean Derome founded the Ensemble de Musique Improvisée de Montréal (EMIM), using an anarchist model. There was no list of members, and anyone could claim to be part of the EMIM as long as they played in an improvisational style. The collective lasted quite some time—long enough to witness the defeat of the "Yes" side in the 1980 referendum and the PQ's subsequent election loss—without particularly making any progress beyond the narrow circles it usually played to. The reason? According to Derome, the obvious relation between Quebec's political culture and its musical culture. "In a certain way, the PQ's failure was written in the musical form it worked in," he said in 1989, going out on a limb. He deplored the importance the Ministry of Cultural Affairs gave to folklore (a music frozen in time) and French-language rock (most of the time imitating American models). He added, "There won't be any change in Quebec as long as people are not […] ready to change the music they listen to and the arts […] they consume."[7] In 2012, after another referendum, two more PQ governments, and the noisy casserole concerts of the student protests, he would put forward the same idea. The future is not written, he implied, thus urging us to live and play that way.[8]

If anything is left of the student demonstrations of spring 2012 (known in Quebec as the Maple Spring), it is the way that art was mobilized to bring the debates into the public sphere. Think of the graphic works by the École de la Montagne Rouge and the Lipdub Rouge clip, as well as the performances by students dressed in red who, through their presence in the Montreal subway system, created parallel communication networks that established dialogues with riders. Most of all, there were the casserole concerts organized spontaneously to protest Bill 78 and its anti-demonstration clauses. Halfway between civil disobedience and carnival procession, this charivari was sometimes accompanied by simultaneous concerts from outdoor balconies, as well as in the alleys and on the main stage of the Francofolies the evening of rap group Loco Locass's performance at the festival.[9] What did all this uproar mean? The art of noise (the casserole players and Jazz Libre alike) is both the precursor and vector of change. In *Noise: The Political Economy of Music*, Jacques Attali writes:

> More than colors and forms, it is sounds and their arrangements that fashion societies. With noise is born disorder and its opposite: the world. With music is born power and its opposite: subversion. In noise can be read the codes of life, the relations

> among men. Clamor, Melody, Dissonance, Harmony: when it is fashioned by man with specific tools, when it invades man's time, when it becomes a sound, noise is the source of power and purpose, of the dream—Music. [10]

Contrary to the casserole bangers, Jazz Libre's cacophony can be listened to and appreciated if a person's ears and mind are a little bit open. And if one hears only sour notes, it could mean that the time has come to imagine new forms of engaged, active listening. The instigators of these sounds, whether they occur in impromptu fashion or as a vocation, like Jazz Libre, are accomplishing important cultural action. Let's listen to it and keep it in our memories; it will help us interpret what is being played at the moment when it counts.

Improvisation is wholly relevant to this story. Jazz Libre was not just theorizing when it presented its work as a social practice. The group might have run into incomprehension, but it was on the right track. Their made-in-Quebec free jazz created new experiences in communication. It was neither nostalgia nor escape. It established in the present moment, in real time, a space for expression that was unique and in perpetual evolution. Improvisation in music demands active listening and an openness to dialogue, trust, cooperation, a free mind, a sense of initiative, the ability to engage in self-criticism, a certain taste for risk, and, of course, a creative disposition to make decisions on a dime and anticipate what might happen next. Given its virtues, improvisation necessarily goes beyond the borders of music. In recent years, efforts have been made to understand its application to other areas and to study it as a complex social phenomenon that can generate new concepts of identity, community, and history in an interconnected world. The engine of politico-cultural revolt, the bearer of collective utopias, it can serve as a way of creating links between individuals and communities. This need cannot be overstated, considering how important it is, in this country and elsewhere, to fight the reactionary tendencies that continue to damage our social fabric. This is how collective, free improvisation finds its community making function, beyond the Marxist, nationalist limits of Jazz Libre. Go ahead, play free—you too!

# Photos and Illustrations

Jazz Libre in 1967. From left to right: Yves Charbonneau, Jean Préfontaine, Guy Thouin, and Maurice Richard. Courtesy of CULSC.

Jazz Libre during the winter of 1969. From left to right: Guy Thouin, Jacques Valois, Yves Charbonneau, Gaby Johnston, and Jean Préfontaine. Courtesy of CULSC.

Poster for the Val-David arts colony.
Courtesy of CULSC.

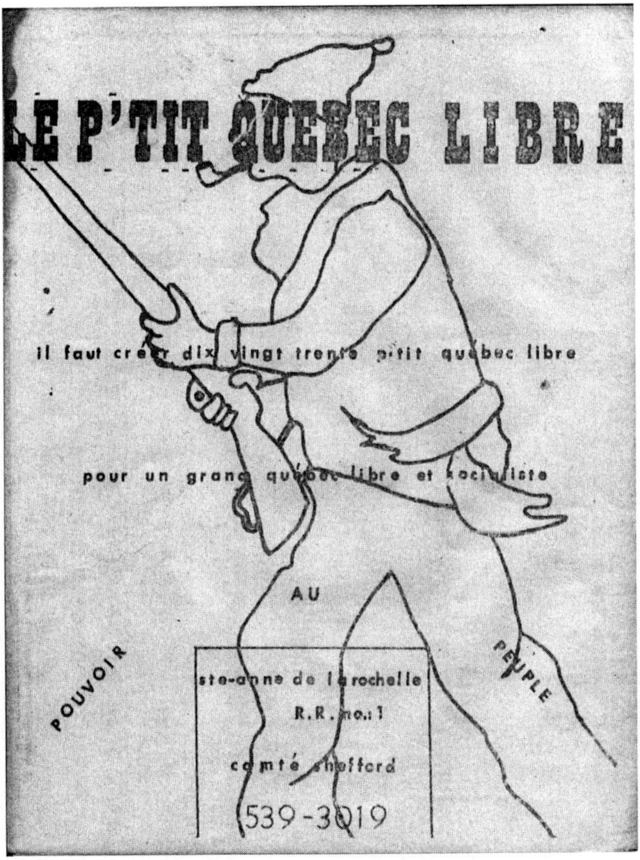


The cover of one of the issues of *Le P'tit Québec libre*.
Courtesy of Tenzier, with permission from Diane Dupuis.

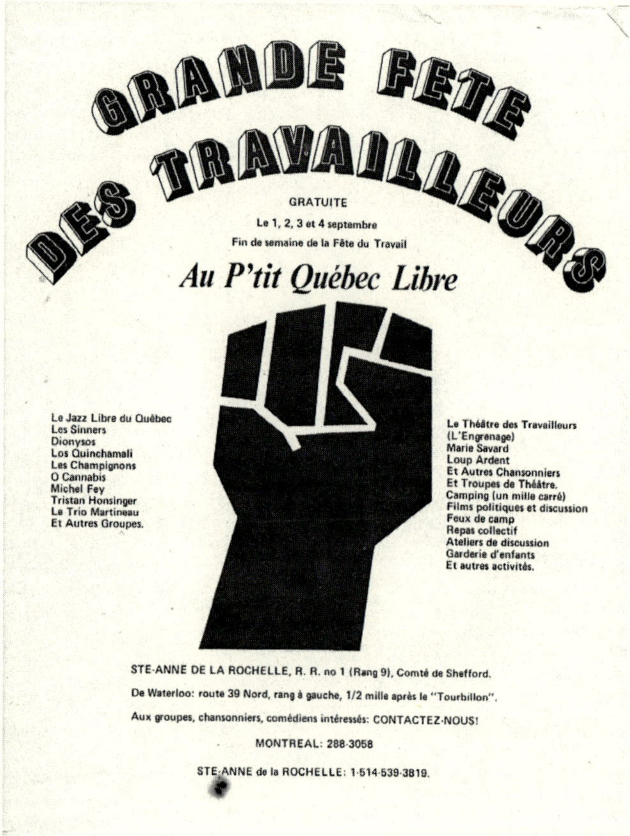


Poster for the 1972 Labour Day festival held at Petit Québec Libre. Courtesy of Tenzier, with permission from Diane Dupuis.

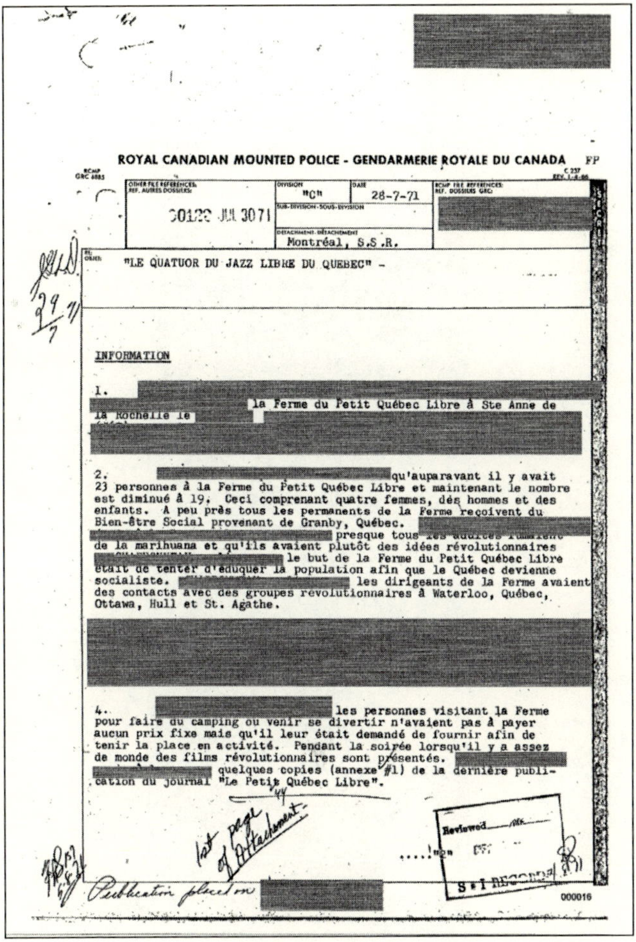

ROYAL CANADIAN MOUNTED POLICE - GENDARMERIE ROYALE DU CANADA

| OTHER FILE REFERENCES / REF. AUTRES DOSSIERS | DIVISION | DATE | RCMP FILE REFERENCES / REF. DOSSIERS GRC |
| --- | --- | --- | --- |
| 30120 JUL 3071 | "C" | 28-7-71 | |
| | SUB-DIVISION - SOUS-DIVISION | | |
| | DETACHMENT - DÉTACHEMENT: Montréal, S.S.R. | | |

RE: / OBJET: "LE QUATUOR DU JAZZ LIBRE DU QUEBEC" -

INFORMATION

1. la Ferme du Petit Québec Libre à Ste Anne de la Rochelle le

2. qu'auparavant il y avait 23 personnes à la Ferme du Petit Québec Libre et maintenant le nombre est diminué à 19. Ceci comprenant quatre femmes, des hommes et des enfants. A peu près tous les permanents de la Ferme reçoivent du Bien-être Social provenant de Granby, Québec. presque tous les adultes fumaient de la marihuana et qu'ils avaient plutôt des idées révolutionnaires le but de la Ferme du Petit Québec Libre était de tenter d'éduquer la population afin que le Québec devienne socialiste. les dirigeants de la Ferme avaient des contacts avec des groupes revolutionnaires à Waterloo, Québec, Ottawa, Hull et St. Agathe.

4. les personnes visitant la Ferme pour faire du camping ou venir se divertir n'avaient pas à payer aucun prix fixe mais qu'il leur était demandé de fournir afin de tenir la place en activité. Pendant la soirée lorsqu'il y a assez de monde des films révolutionnaires sont présentés. quelques copies (annexe #1) de la dernière publication du journal "Le Petit Québec Libre".

1st page of Attachment.

Publication placed on

Reviewed

S I RECORD

000016

Royal Canadian Mounted Police surveillance report (file A-2014-00485 / © Government of Canada). Courtesy of Library and Archives Canada.

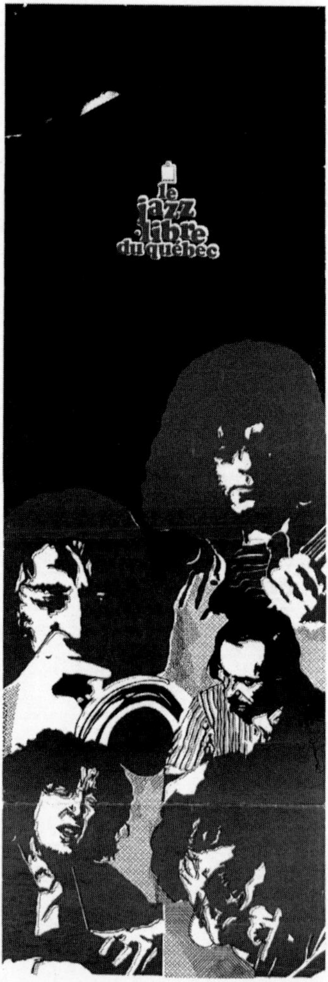


Poster designed by Pierre Monat for Jazz Libre's 1972 Local Initiatives Program tour (LIP).
Courtesy of CULSC, with permission from Pierre Monat.

Poster for the two concerts that Jazz Libre gave in Italy in 1973.
Courtesy of CULSC.

The fire at L'Amorce in June of 1974.
Courtesy of the Montreal Firefighters Museum.

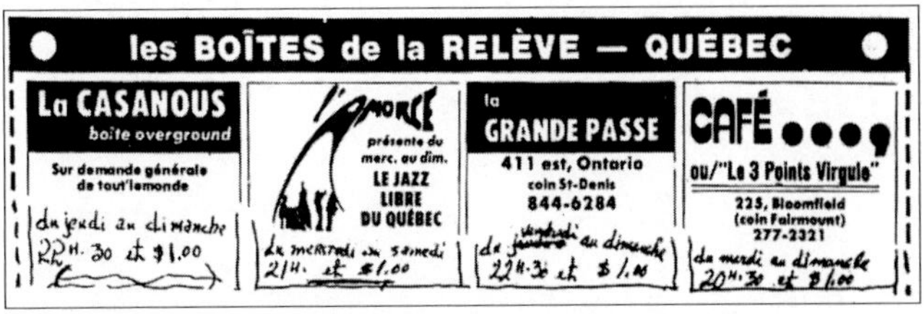


Advertisement in *Mainmise* for the parallel circuit of creative centres that Jazz Libre helped establish.
Courtesy of BAnQ.

Jazz Libre at the Centre d'Essai le Conventum after the fire that destroyed L'Amorce in 1974. From left to right: Yves Charbonneau, Mathieu Léger, and Maurice Richard.
Courtesy of photographer Errol Gagné.

# Notes

## PREFACE

1 John Norris, "CBC," *Coda* 10, no. 8 (July/August 1972): 9.

2 Chris Kennedy, "Le Quatuor de jazz libre du Québec, 1973," *Musicworks*, no. 113 (Summer 2012): 58.

3 Marc Chénard, "Free Jazz Then … and Now," *La Scena Musicale* 17, no. 6 (March 2012): 30.

4 Stuart Broomer, "Musique-Politique: Anthologie 1971–1974," *The WholeNote* 25, no. 2 (October 2019): 73. Listen to Quatuor de jazz libre du Québec, *S/T*, London Records of Canada/Radio-Canada International, NAS 13515, 33⅓ rpm, 1969, LP; Quatuor de jazz libre du Québec, *1973*, Tenzier, TNZR051, 33⅓ rpm, 2011, LP; Quatuor de jazz libre du Québec, *S/T*, Return to Analog Records, RTA-029, 33⅓ rpm, 2018, LP; and Quatuor de jazz libre du Québec, *Musique-Politique: Anthologie 1971/1974*, Tour de bras, TDBHIST0001, 4XCD, 2019.

5 Ajay Heble, *Landing on the Wrong Note: Jazz, Discourse, and Critical Practice* (Routledge: New York, 2000), 28.

## INTRODUCTION

1 Cited in Jacques Larue-Langlois, "Une musique jaillie de l'âme québécoise," *La Presse*, May 10, 1969, 21.

2 A literal translation of the term "free jazz," Jazz Libre was the name that people commonly used when referring to the group. It was a convenient shorthand considering the name's many variations between 1967 and 1975. These reflected the changes in personnel and the different stages of the group's approach to music and politics: Quatuor du Nouveau Jazz Libre du Québec, Quatuor de Jazz Libre du Québec, Jazz Libre du Québec, Rock Libre du Québec, Communards du P'tit Québec Libre, and Jazz Lib' du Kebek. I use "Jazz Libre" in this book for ease of reading.

3 Raoul Roy, "Québec est une colonie! Sus au colonialisme!," *La Revue socialiste*, no. 6 (Fall 1962): 5.

4 André D'Allemagne, *Le colonialisme au Québec* (Montreal: Éditions R-B, 1966).

5 "Présentation," *Parti pris* 1, no. 1 (October 1963): 4.

6 As a concept, "decolonizing socialism" provided a helpful framework for the social, political, and cultural theories that filled the pages of *Parti pris*. See, for example, Paul Chamberland, "Aliénation culturelle et révolution nationale," *Parti pris* 1, no. 2 (November 1963): 10–22.

7 As in the subtitle of Pierre Vallières, *Nègres blancs d'Amérique: Autobiographie précoce d'un "terroriste" québécois* (Montreal: Parti pris, 1968), translated into English as Pierre Vallières, *White Niggers of America: The Precocious Autobiography of a Quebec "Terrorist,"* trans. Joan Pinkham (New York: [Monthly Review Press], 1971).

8 The following call to action appears on the cover of many issues of *Le P'tit Québec libre*, the commune's newspaper: "We have to establish ten, twenty, thirty Petit Québec Libre to bring about a larger, free, socialist Quebec." See Chapter 4 for details about this publication.

9 LeRoi Jones, *Blues People: Negro Music in White America* (New York: Perennial, 2002), 235.

10 Frank Kofsky, *Black Nationalism and the Revolution in Music* (New York: Pathfinder Press, 1970), 131.

11 Cited in Philippe Carles and Jean-Louis Comolli, *Free Jazz/Black Power*, trans. Grégory Pierrot (Jackson: University Press of Mississippi, 2015), 175.

12 Jean-Louis Comolli, "Voyage au bout de la new thing," *Jazz Magazine*, no. 129 (April 1966): 27. See also Carles and Comolli, *Free Jazz/Black Power*, 175–79.

13 Patrick Straram, "Les divertissements: Jazz dans la vie quotidienne," *Parti pris* 1, no. 3 (December 1963): 55.

14 Patrick Straram, "Jazz dans la vie quotidienne: Comparaisons," *Parti pris* 1, no. 7 (April 1964): 52.

15 Patrick Straram, "Tea for One 2 Hypojazz," in *Musique du Kébèk*, ed. Raôul Duguay (Montreal: Éditions du jour, 1971), 246.

16 Guy Thouin, interview with author, August 29, 2011.

17 Cited in Jacques Thériault, "Le Quatuor du nouveau jazz libre du Québec," *Le Devoir*, January 20, 1968, 11.

18 Jean Préfontaine, "Jazz libre = Musique-action," in *Musique du Kébèk*, ed. Raôul Duguay (Montreal: Éditions du Jour, 1971), 164.

19 Ibid., 157.

20 In reference to Sean Mills, *The Empire Within: Postcolonial Thought and Political Activism in Sixties Montreal* (Montreal: McGill-Queen's University Press, 2010).

21 Yves Robillard et al., *Québec underground, 1962–1972—Tome I* (Montreal: Médiart, 1973), 394.

22 Jean Préfontaine (1926–2008), Maurice Richard (1946–2002), and Guy Thouin (1940–) founded Jazz Libre with Yves Charbonneau (1934–2007) in 1967. Préfontaine and Charbonneau formed the central core of the group during its eight years of existence. Pierre Nadeau (piano), Gaby Johnston (saxophone), Tristan Honsinger (cello), Jacques Valois (bass), Jean Martineau (bass and guitar), Jacques Beaudoin (bass), Yves Bouliane (bass), Cyril Lepage (drums), Curly Virgil (drums), Jean-Guy Poirier (drums), Patrice Beckerich (drums), and Mathieu Léger (drums) joined Jazz Libre at different moments between 1967 and 1975.

## CHAPTER ONE

1 Emmanuel Cocke, "Le Quatuor du nouveau jazz libre du Québec," *Ciné-Jazz*, no. 1 (1968): 33.

2 Emmanuel Cocke, "Jazz et variétés: Quatuor du nouveau jazz libre du Québec," n.d., article, Jean Préfontaine Fonds (JPF), Concordia University Library Special Collections (CULSC).

3 Thériault, "Le Quatuor du nouveau jazz libre du Québec," 11.

4 See Paul-Émile Borduas, *Total Refusal: The Complete 1948 Manifesto of the Montreal Automatists*, trans. Ray Ellenwood (Toronto: Exile Editions, 1985).

5 Louis Gill, *Art, politique, révolution: Manifeste pour l'indépendance de l'art* (Montreal: M Éditeur, 2012), 132.

6 Claude Gingras, "Jazz et chanson à la nouvelle Anse," *La Presse*, April 5, 1968, 10.

7 Jean Préfontaine to John Gilmore, December 4, 1985, JPF, CULSC.

8 The guitarist Paul Morin would have also joined the group for a few weeks in Pointe-Calumet.

9 Préfontaine, "Jazz libre = Musique-action," 164.

10 John Gilmore, *Swinging in Paradise: The Story of Jazz in Montreal* (Montreal: Véhicule Press, 1988), 245–46.

11 Thériault, "Le Quatuor du nouveau jazz libre du Québec," 11.

12 Cocke, "Le Quatuor du nouveau jazz libre du Québec," 34.

13 Gilles Ouellet, "Dans le sillage des grands démons noirs du jazz libre," *La Presse*, October 21, 1967, 22.

14 Cocke, "Jazz et variétés."

15 Gilmore, *Swinging in Paradise*, 321.

16 Ouellet, "Dans le sillage des grands démons noirs du jazz libre," 22.

17 Cited in Gilles Ouellet, "Walter Boudreau au premier rang," *La Presse*, November 18, 1967, 24.

18 Walter Boudreau, interview with author, February 23, 2012.

19 Ibid.

20 Ouellet, "Walter Boudreau au premier rang," 24.

21 Thériault, "Le Quatuor du nouveau jazz libre du Québec," 11.

22 Cited in Ouellet, "Dans le sillage des grands démons noirs du jazz libre," 22.

23 Yves Préfontaine, "John Coltrane, une révolte qui bâtit l'homme," *Liberté* 3, no. 6 (December 1961): 797; and Yves Préfontaine, "Musicojazz," *Liberté* 3, nos. 3–4 (May–August 1961): 672.

24 Préfontaine, "Musicojazz," 672.

25 This intertitle appears at the beginning of the film. See Gilles Groulx, *The Cat in the Bag*, National Film Board of Canada, Montreal, 1964, 35 mm.

26 Ibid.

27 Patrick Straram, "Situations d'une critique et d'une production," *Cahier pour un paysage à inventer*, no. 1 (May 1960): 96.

28 Ibid., 70.

29 *Le jazz prend feu*, April 26, 1968, transcription of radio show, Patrick Straram Fonds (PSF), Bibliothèque et Archives nationales du Québec (BAnQ).

30 Patrick Straram, "Bluesologie," *Liberté* 3, no. 2 (March–April 1961): 542.

31 Ibid., 538.

32 Ibid., 542.

33 Yvon Dionne, "Vers une révolte totale," *Parti pris* 1, no. 1 (October 1963): 31.

34 Writing in 1972, the journalist Malcolm Reid wondered about the link between the "angry literature" of each group. "There is surely a common category into which Allen Ginsberg's *Howl* and Paul Chamberland's *hurle* both fall," he noted, hesitant to place too much emphasis on this observation. Malcolm Reid, *The Shouting Signpainters: A Literary and Political Account of Quebec Revolutionary Nationalism* (New York: [Monthly Review Press], 1972), 128.

35 Paul Chamberland, "L'individu révolutionnaire," *Parti pris* 3, no. 5 (December 1965): 17.

36 André Major, "Langagement (1960-1975)," *Voix et Images* 1, no. 1 (1975): 121.

37 Pierre Maheu, "De la révolte à la révolution," *Parti pris* 1, no. 1 (October 1963): 11.

38 Robert Major, *Parti pris: Idéologies et littérature* (Montreal: Cahiers du Québec/Hurtubise HMH, 1979), 18.

39 Maheu, "De la révolte à la révolution," 12.

40 Paul Chamberland, "Dire ce que je suis," *Parti pris* 2, no. 5 (January 1965): 42.

41 Maheu, "De la révolte à la révolution," 12. See also Denys Arcand, "Cinéma et sexualité," *Parti pris* 1, nos. 9–10–11 (Summer 1964): 90.

42 "Manifeste 1965-66," *Parti pris* 6, nos. 1–2 (August–September 1965): 21.

43 Chamberland, "Aliénation culturelle et révolution nationale," 20.

44 Henri Lefebvre, *Critique de la vie quotidienne—Tome 1* (Paris: L'Arche, 1958), 50.

45 Guy Debord, "Perspectives de modifications conscientes dans la vie quotidienne," *Internationale situationniste*, no. 6 (August 1961): 22.

46 Straram, "Bluesologie," 542; Straram, "Les divertissements," 56; Straram, "Jazz dans la vie quotidienne," 52; Patrick Straram, "Les divertissements 3: Jazz dans la vie quotidienne," *Parti pris* 1, no. 5 (February 1964): 58; Patrick Straram, "Interprétation de la vie quotidienne," *Parti pris* 3, no. 5 (December 1965): 65; Straram, "Tea for One 2 Hypojazz," 229.

47 Straram, "Les divertissements," 55.

48 Vallières, *White Niggers of America*, 52–53.

49 Straram, "Tea for One 2 Hypojazz," 223.

50 Ibid., 244.

51 For example, read Robert Tremblay, "Les noirs d'ici," *Parti pris* 5, no. 6 (March 1968): 17–23.

52 David Austin, *Fear of a Black Nation: Race, Sex, and Security in Sixties Montreal* (Toronto: Between the Lines, 2013), 45.

53 Carmel Dumas, *Montréal chaud/show: Chronique libre d'une explosion culturelle* (Montreal: Fides, 2008), 110.

54 Patrick Straram, *Bribes 1: Pré-textes & lectures* (Montreal: L'Aurore, 1975), 47.

55 Pierre Boisvert, "Quatuor du nouveau jazz libre du Québec," *Le Voyage* 1, no. 1 (May 1968): 18.

56 Gilmore, *Swinging in Paradise*, 285.

57 Guy Thouin, interview with author, August 29, 2011.

58 Cocke, "Le Quatuor du nouveau jazz libre du Québec," 33.

## CHAPTER TWO

1 Yves Leclerc, "Le nouveau Charlebois ou la fin tragique de l'Osstidcho," *La Presse*, October 9, 1969, 10.

2 Cited in Cocke, "Le Quatuor du nouveau jazz libre du Québec," 33.

3 Cited in Baptiste Vignol, "Robert Charlebois: Un gars ben ordinaire?," *Schnock*, no. 15 (Summer 2015): 87.

4 Cited in Denise Boucher, "Robert Charlebois ou la chanson coup de poing," *La Presse—Perspectives*, November 9, 1968, 12.

5 Louise Forestier, cited in Bruno Roy, *L'Osstidcho ou le désordre libérateur* (Montreal: XYZ, 2008), 72.

6 In reference to the title of Roy's book.

7 Louise Forestier, interview with author, March 20, 2012.

8 Cited in Dumas, *Montréal chaud/show*, 218.

9 Claude Gingras, "Poèmes et chansons de la 'résistance au colonialisme,'" *La Presse*, May 22, 1968, 72.

10 Claude Gingras, "Poèmes et chansons de la résistance," *La Presse*, May 28, 1968, 69.

11 Ibid.

12 Gingras, "Folie partielle, musicale et verbale…," *La Presse*, May 29, 1968, 63.

13 Claude Gingras, "'Happening' à la Comédie-Canadienne," *La Presse*, September 3, 1968, 28.

14 Louise Forestier, interview with author, March 20, 2012.

15 See record liner notes by Edward Farrant on the back cover of Quatuor de jazz libre du Québec, *S/T*, London Records of Canada/Radio-Canada International, NAS 13515, 33⅓ rpm, 1969, LP.

16 Guy Thouin, interview with author, February 21, 2012.

17 Louise Forestier, *Forestier selon Louise: Pas d'choker, pas d'collier* (Montreal: Éditions La Presse, 2011), 97.

18 Danièle Heymann, "Les Canadiens ont étranglé Maria Chapdelaine," *L'Express*, April 7–13, 1969, 52.

19 Forestier, *Forestier selon Louise*, 97.

20 Suzanne Thomas, "Robert Charlebois et Louise

Forestier doivent quitter l'Olympia avant la fin de leur engagement," *La Patrie*, April 13, 1969, 3.

21 See the first page of the April 13, 1969, edition of *La Patrie*.

22 René Homier-Roy, "Charlebois est mis à la porte de l'Olympia," *La Presse*, April 11, 1969, 1.

23 *À soir on fait peur au monde*, n.d., promotional pamphlet from the Conseil québécois pour la diffusion du cinéma, Médiathèque Guy-L.-Coté (Cinémathèque québécoise).

24 Guy Latraverse, *50 ans de showbiz québécois* (Montreal: Éditions La Presse, 2013), 90.

25 Cited in Dumas, *Montréal chaud/show*, 253.

26 Claudine Monfette, interview with author, December 21, 2015.

27 Jean Préfontaine to John Gilmore, December 4, 1985, JPF, CULSC.

28 Cited in Boucher, "Robert Charlebois ou la chanson coup de poing," 8.

29 Leclerc, "Le nouveau Charlebois ou la fin tragique de l'Osstidcho," 10.

30 Robert Charlebois, interview with author, May 3, 2016.

31 Cited in Dumas, *Montréal chaud/show*, 246.

32 Ibid. Regarding Robidoux and his role as a "musical reconciler," see the credits for Robert Charlebois and Louise Forestier, *S/T*, Gamma, GS-120, 33⅓ rpm, 1968, LP.

33 Roy, *L'Osstidcho ou le désordre libérateur*, 19–21.

34 Jean-Pierre Sirois-Trahan, "L'évolution intranquille: Multiplicité et rock québécois," in *La contre-culture au Québec*, eds. Karim Larose and Frédéric Rondeau (Montreal: Presses de l'Université de Montréal, 2016), 71.

35 Patrick Straram is referring here to Michel Garneau, Paul-Marie Lapointe, Yves Préfontaine, and Michel van Schendel, among others. He would subsequently write that a "fruitful and fascinating study could be made about jazz and its relationship to the works of Paul Chamberland, Gérald Godin, Réjean Ducharme, Roland Giguère, Jacques Renaud." Straram,

"Les divertissements," 55; Straram, "Tea for One 2 Hypojazz," 250.

36 "L'amour suprême," October 26, 1967, concert program, Walter Boudreau Fonds (WBF), CULSC.

37 Raôul Duguay, "Or art (poésie) total du cri au chant au," *Quoi* 1, no. 2 (1967): 13.

38 Thérèse Dumouchel, "Les arts zartistiques," *Parti pris* 5, no. 1 (September 1967): 57.

39 See Pierre Maheu, "La poésie rebelle de Raôul Duguay," *Parti pris* 5, no. 6 (March 1968): 51–53.

40 Cited in Robillard et al., *Québec underground*, 414.

41 Ibid.

42 Marcel Saint-Pierre, "Les arts en spectacle," in *Les arts visuels au Québec dans les années soixante. Tome II: L'éclatement du modernisme*, ed. Francine Couture (Montreal: VLB Éditeur, 1997), 84.

43 Paul Chamberland, "Faire le voyage. Entretien avec Claude Péloquin," *Parti pris* 3, no. 9 (April 1966): 40.

44 *Le Carnet des arts*, July 10, 1968, transcription of radio show, WBF, CULSC.

45 Claude St-Germain (aka Edualk Ts-Naimreg) was the group's "storyteller." See the personnel list for L'Infonie, *Vol. 33: Mantra*, Polydor, 2424 018, 33 rpm, 1970, LP.

46 Jacques Valois, interview with author, May 10, 2012.

47 "L'Infonie et Walter Boudreau veulent aller plus loin que Robert Charlebois," n.d., article, WBF, CULSC.

48 Raôul Duguay, *Manifeste de L'Infonie: Le ToutArtBel* (Montreal: Éditions du Jour, 1970), 101.

49 "L'Infonie: 17 maniaques en liberté!," n.d., article, WBF, CULSC.

50 Cited in Duguay, *Manifeste de L'Infonie*, 27.

51 Ibid., 21.

52 Alfred Willi Rudolf "Rudi" Dutschke survived this attempt on his life. Wishes of a speedy recovery appeared in the pages of *Parti pris*. Patrick Straram, "À la santé de Rudi Dutschke et quelques autres folk-rock mirabellenwasser," *Parti pris* 5, no. 8 (Summer 1968): 65–72.

53 Jules Duchastel, "La contre-culture, une idéologie de l'apolitisme," in *La transformation du pouvoir au Québec. Actes du colloque de l'ACSALF (1979)*, ed. Association canadienne des sociologues et anthropologues de langue française (Montreal: Éditions Albert Saint-Martin, 1980), 256.

54 "Alternative" was the term that many of the authors who contributed to *Mainmise* used to describe the wide array of discourses and practices associated with the counterculture. See Pénélope, "Pénélope et le Québec alternatif," *Mainmise*, no. 3 (1971): 42.

55 Duguay, *Manifeste de L'Infonie*, 33.

56 See Préfontaine's liner notes on the back cover of Quatuor de jazz libre du Québec, *S/T*, London Records of Canada/Radio-Canada International, NAS 13515, 33⅓ rpm, 1969, LP.

57 Cited in Jean Basile, "L'Infonie vous aime (quand même)," *Le Devoir*, March 7, 1970, 11.

58 Ibid.

59 Louise Tassé, "L'Infonie accepte tout pour tout changer," n.d., article, WBF, CULSC.

60 Cited in Larue-Langlois, "Une musique jaillie de l'âme québécoise," 21.

61 Guy Thouin, interview with author, February 21, 2012.

62 Cited in Larue-Langlois, "Une musique jaillie de l'âme québécoise," 21.

## CHAPTER THREE

1 Pierre Cadieux, "Le Jazz libre du Québec c'est quecchose de spécial," *Quartier latin* 52, no. 13 (March 12–29, 1970), 29.

2 Cited in Robillard et al., *Québec underground*, 204.

3 Anithe de Carvalho, *Art rebelle et contre-culture: Création collective underground au Québec* (Montreal: M Éditeur, 2015), 119.

4 Richard Lacroix, interview with author, June 24, 2015.

5 Cited in Robillard et al., *Québec underground*, 248.

6 Ibid., 291.

7 Ibid., 319.

8 Ibid.

9 Ibid., 155.

10 Cocke, "Le Quatuor du nouveau jazz libre du Québec," 34.

11 Richard Lacroix, interview with author, June 24, 2015.

12 "Deux jours d'animation culturelle," n.d., project abstract, JPF, CULSC.

13 These are the terms used by the collective to describe the project. See Fernand Dansereau, *Jonquière*, Radio-Canada, Montreal, 1969, video.

14 Ibid.

15 Cadieux, "Le Jazz libre du Québec c'est quecchose de spécial," 29.

16 Jean Préfontaine to M. Valier Savoie, May 28, 1968, JPF, CULSC.

17 Jean Préfontaine to Gilbert Comtois, August 15, 1968, JPF, CULSC.

18 Jacques Valois, interview with author, May 10, 2012.

19 Diane Dupuis, interview with author, April 7, 2012.

20 JLQ-P-1994-0014-0099-A-1-A-2-L, February 4, 1973, recording of a concert in Montreal, Jazz Libre Collection (JLC), Centre Tenzier pour la préservation et la diffusion des avant-gardes québécoises (Tenzier); JLQ-P-1994-0014-0084-B-1-B-2.R, June 20, 1970, recording of a concert in Grand-Mère, JLC, Tenzier.

21 JLQ-P-110872-AdJ-Drummondville-M, August 11, 1972, recording of a concert in Drummondville, JLC, Tenzier.

22 Préfontaine, "Jazz libre = Musique-action," 165.

23 JLQ-P-1994-0014-0099-A-1-A-2-L, February 4, 1973, recording of a concert in Montreal, JLC, Tenzier.

24 Thériault, "Le Quatuor du nouveau jazz libre du Québec," 11.

25 Ulysse, "Le rock est-il fait pour les sourds?," *Mainmise*, no. 3 (1971): 88.

26 Marie-France Thériault, "Mainmise: Trois ans de recherche," *Mainmise*, no. 26 (August 1973): 29; Ulysse, "Le rock est-il fait pour les sourds?," 91.

27 Aaron Howard, "Rock," *Logos* 2, no. 3 (August 1969): 1.

28 "2—musique," *Mainmise*, no. 4 (April 1971): 158; "La musique du colon," *Mainmise*, no. 23 (May 1973): 39.

29 Richard Thérien, "Le jazz, qu'est-ce que c'est?," *Mainmise*, no. 27 (September 1973): 88–95.

30 Ibid., 95.

31 Préfontaine, "Jazz libre = Musique-action," 163–64.

32 Yves Charbonneau and Jean Préfontaine, "Sherbrooke, festival pop," *Le P'tit Québec libre*, no. 7 (July 2, 1971): 6.

33 Esperanto Allary, "The Music Corporation: A Few Negative Remarks," *Logos* 3, no. 3 (June 1970): 19.

34 "Pour un Front de libération du rock," *Mainmise*, no. 9 (December 1971): 225.

35 "Projet d'une colonie artistique," n.d., project description, JPF, CULSC.

36 *Quotidien*, n.d., draft version of a publication for the arts colony, inserted in the reel-to-reel box JLQ-P-1994-0014-0096, July 1970, JLC, Tenzier.

37 Françoise Labonne, interview with author, May 22, 2012.

38 "La Colonie artistique de Val-David," n.d., poster, JPF, CULSC.

39 Cited in Andrée Gauthier, "Un jazzman d'ici dans la métropole," *Le Progrès du golfe*, March 23, 1967, 16.

40 JLQ-P-1994-0014-0084-B-1-B-2.R, June 20, 1970, recording of a concert in Grand-Mère, JLC, Tenzier.

41 This is the name that reporters gave to the festival: "À Val-David, un festival pop anti-capitaliste," *Journal de Montréal*, September 2, 1970, 4.

42 "La colonie," *La Claque*, no. 1 (1970): 2.

43 Report no. 177030970015, September 4, 1970, Opération Festival de musique de Val-David, Sûreté du Québec Fonds (SQF), BAnQ.

44 Report from Jean-Luc Paquin, n.d., Opération Festival pop de Manseau, SQF, BAnQ.

45 Report from Robert Turpin, August 17, 1970, Opération Festival pop de Manseau, SQF, BAnQ.

46 Report no. 177030970015, September 4, 1970, Opération Festival de musique de Val-David, SQF, BAnQ.

47 Ibid.

48 Gilles Normand, "Le groupe 'Jazz libre du Québec' se dit harcelé par la police," *La Presse*, September 5, 1970, 3.

49 Report no. 177030970015, September 4, 1970, Opération Festival de musique de Val-David, SQF, BAnQ.

50 Jean Préfontaine and Yves Charbonneau, "L'Aventure socialiste du Jazz libre du Québec," *Quartier latin* 53, no. 4 (October 24 – November 6, 1970): 28.

51 Cited in Jean-Claude Trait, "Festival de la fraternité: Plus de 3,000 jeunes à Val David," *La Presse*, September 8, 1970, 10.

52 Préfontaine and Charbonneau, "L'Aventure socialiste du Jazz libre du Québec," 28.

53 Ibid.

54 Ibid.

## CHAPTER FOUR

1 Jean Basile, "Une initiative du Jazz libre du Québec," *Le Devoir*, January 28, 1971, 10.

2 "Le P'tit Q libre: Centre d'activités socioculturelles et de formation politique," n.d., leaflet, Yves Charbonneau Fonds (YCF), CULSC.

3 Ibid.

4 "Projet du P'tit Québec libre," n.d., project description, YCF, CULSC.

5 Diane Dupuis, interview with author, April 7, 2012. See also draft of an undated essay by Yves Charbonneau on the history of the commune, YCF, CULSC.

6 Curly Virgil's mandate as a drummer was to lend a helping hand to Jazz Libre in the closing days of the arts colony in Val-David. He did not accompany the group to Sainte-Anne-de-la-Rochelle.

7 Préfontaine and Charbonneau, "L'Aventure socialiste du Jazz libre du Québec," 28.

8 "Travailleurs québécois! Le Petit Québec libre c'est à vous autres," *Le P'tit Québec libre*, no. 1 (May 24, 1971): 1.

9 "Projet de la ferme du Jazz libre du Québec," November 1970, project description, YCF, CULSC.

10 "Projet du P'tit Québec libre," n.d., project description, YCF, CULSC.

11 Completed in 1970, Denys Arcand's film was censored by its producer, the National Film Board of Canada. Bootleg copies on video nonetheless circulated until the film was finally released in 1976. Réal La Rochelle, "Arcand, Denys (1941–)," in *Dictionnaire de la censure au Québec*, eds. Pierre Hébert, Yves Lever, and Kenneth Landry (Montreal: Fides, 2006), 45–50.

12 "Projet du P'tit Québec libre," n.d., project description, YCF, CULSC.

13 Yves Charbonneau and Jean Préfontaine, "Une nouvelle musique populaire," *Le P'tit Québec libre*, no. 1 (May 24, 1971): 7. The two had to hire musicians in the early days of the commune. Jazz Libre then found itself on hiatus until it could recruit new members on the eve of obtaining a grant from the Local Initiatives Program, which I discuss in Chapter 5.

14 François Mario Bachand, *Trois textes* (Montreal: n.p., 1972), 167.

15 *Manifeste du Petit Québec libre*, n.d., manifesto, JPF, CULSC.

16 The name of the commune's publication is sometimes spelled *Le Petit Québec libre*.

17 This statement appears on the cover of the first issue of *Le P'tit Québec libre*, dated May 24, 1971.

18 "Les coopératives et la révolution," *Le P'tit Québec libre*, no. 6 (June 24, 1971): 2.

19 "Nos droits et nos devoirs en cas d'arrestation," *Le P'tit Québec libre*, no. 7 (July 2, 1971): 4.

20 "Qu'ossé qu'on fait?!!," *Le P'tit Québec libre*, no. 1 (May 24, 1971): 6.

21 "1837–1971...," *Le P'tit Québec libre*, n.d. The image of the "old patriot" derives from a sketch by Henri Julien (circa 1880).

22 "Demande de cotisation adressée aux syndicats et

aux fédérations pour le P'tit Québec libre," January 13, 1971, newsletter, JPF, CULSC.

23 Fernand Foisy, interview with author, May 22, 2012.

24 "Résolution du comité exécutif du CCSNM pour l'indépendance du Québec, n.d., Dossier Congrès 1972 (DC72), Confédération des syndicats nationaux, Service des communications (CSN-SC).

25 "La démocratie culturelle," n.d., excerpt from the Déclaration de principes du CCSNM, DC72, CSN-SC.

26 "Rapport de Victor Leroux," n.d., Dossier Congrès 1971 (DC71). CSN-SC.

27 "La démocratie culturelle," n.d., excerpt from the Déclaration de principes du CCSNM, DC72, CSN-SC.

28 "Rapport du secrétaire (Annexe 006—Le Théâtre des travailleurs)," n.d., DC72, CSN-SC.

29 Jean-Pierre Compain, *L'Engrenage: Tremplin pour une socialisation des arts et de la culture* (Montreal: L'Étincelle, 1972), 31. See also "Le Théâtre des travailleurs: 1970," *Jeu: Revue de théâtre*, no. 7 (1978): 38–42.

30 The "Lapalme guys" were postal workers who saw their contract with the Canadian government cancelled at the beginning of 1970. The group's struggle against their former employer received the support of many radical organizations, including the FLQ. See Pierre Vadeboncoeur, *366 jours et tant qu'il en faudra. Vive les gars de Lapalme!* (Montreal: Confédération des syndicats nationaux, 1971).

31 Compain, *L'Engrenage*, 32.

32 Cited in Louis Fournier, *FLQ: Histoire d'un mouvement clandestin* (Montreal: Lanctôt Éditeur, 1998), 196.

33 Austin, *Fear of a Black Nation*, 137.

34 Mills, *The Empire Within*, 7.

35 The two musicians suspected that Daniel Waterlot was not entirely trustworthy and that he occasionally lied about things—which explains their decision to remain autonomous from organizations such as the Communist Party of Quebec. Diane Dupuis, interview with author, April 7, 2012.

36 Jean-Philippe Warren, *Ils voulaient changer le monde: Le militantisme marxiste-léniniste au Québec* (Montreal: VLB Éditeur, 2007), 21.

37 "Le camp du P'tit Québec libre, une autre Maison du pêcheur," *La Patrie*, July 11, 1971, 10.

38 Jacques Maher, "Le Petit Québec libre: une maison de pêcheurs à 60 milles de Montréal," *Le Petit journal*, May 16, 1971, 2.

39 Canada, House of Commons Debates, 28th Parliament, 3rd Session, Vol. 7, June 28, 1971, Léonel Beaudoin, 7377.

40 Maher, "Le Petit Québec libre," 2.

41 JLQ-P-1994-014-0126-A-1-A-2-L, July 22, 1972, recording of a performance at Petit Québec libre, JLC, Tenzier.

42 JLQ-P-1994-014-0125, July 8, 1972, recording of a performance at Petit Québec libre, JLC, Tenzier.

43 Ibid.

44 "Rumeurs, rumeurs, rumeurs," *Le P'tit Québec libre*, no. 7 (July 2, 1971): 2.

45 "Le P'tit Québec libre et les mass-média," n.d., draft of article for *Le P'tit Québec libre*, JLC, Tenzier.

46 "Le nudisme au P.Q.L.," *Le P'tit Québec libre*, no. 7 (July 2, 1971): 2.

47 Paule Courtois, "Le P'tit Québec libre: Une ferme vacances où cultiver ses talents," *La Presse—Perspectives*, March 13, 1971, 12.

48 "La prochaine fois… nous vaincrons," n.d., draft of article for *Le P'tit Québec libre*, JLC, Tenzier.

49 "Projet du P'tit Québec libre," n.d., project description, YCF, CULSC.

50 JLQ-P-1994-014-0126-A-1-A-2-L, July 22, 1972, recording of a performance at Petit Québec libre, JLC, Tenzier.

51 "La voix des prisons," *Le P'tit Québec libre*, no. 9 (n.d.): 2.

52 Ibid.

53 "Pourquoi la libération des femmes," *Le P'tit Québec libre*, no. 4 (n.d.): 1.

54 See Véronique O'Leary and Louise Toupin, eds., *Québécoises deboutte! Tome 1* (Montreal: Remue-ménage, 1982), 83.

55 "Pourquoi la libération des femmes," 1.

56 Cited in Maher, "Le Petit Québec libre," 2.

57 Diane Dupuis, interview with author, April 7, 2012.

58 See draft of an undated essay by Yves Charbonneau on the history of the commune, YCF, CULSC.

59 Cited in Maher, "Le Petit Québec Libre," 2.

60 "Le P'tit Québec libre," *Deux mai* 2, no. 14 (April 1971): 11–12.

61 Pénélope, "Pénélope et le Québec alternatif," 42–51.

62 Pénélope, "Et maintenant Pénélope vous parle de *Mainmise* 5," *Mainmise*, no. 5 (1971): 15; Pénélope, "Et maintenant Pénélope vous parle de *Mainmise* qui a 1 an," *Mainmise*, no. 6 (1971): 19.

63 "La naissance d'un nouvel homme québécois," *Le P'tit Québec libre*, no. 1 (May 24, 1971): 2.

64 Steve Kowch, "Radicals Met Near Barn Before Mounties Burned It," *The Gazette*, November 4, 1977, 4.

65 See "Rapport de la Gendarmerie royale du Canada sur 'La Maison du Chômeur,' St-Hyacinthe," June 8, 1971, Canadian Security Intelligence Service Fonds (CSISF), Library and Archives Canada (LAC); "Rapport de la Gendarmerie royale du Canada sur la 'Ferme du P'tit Québec libre,'" July 16, 1971, CSISF, LAC; "Rapport de la Gendarmerie royale du Canada sur 'La Maison du Chômeur,' Saint-Hyacinthe," August 5, 1971, CSISF, LAC; "Rapport de la Gendarmerie royale du Canada sur 'Le Quatuor du jazz libre du Québec,'" July 28, 1971; and "Rapport de la Gendarmerie royale du Canada sur les activités du 'Front de libération québécois,'" July 22, 1971. See also "District de Montréal—Surveillance du territoire—Dossiers opérationnels (1972–1991)," volume 2007-05-010/41, SQF, BAnQ; and "Enlèvement et meurtre—Affaires Cross et Laporte (1970)," volume 2006-04-003/200, SQF, BAnQ.

66 Cited in Fournier, *FLQ*, 279.

67 See draft of an undated essay by Yves Charbonneau on the history of the commune, YCF, CULSC.

68 Kowch, "Radicals Met Near Barn Before Mounties Burned It," 4.

69 *Rapport de la Commission d'enquête sur des opérations*

*policières en territoire québécois* (Quebec City: Ministère de la Justice, 1981), 327.

70 The four police officers were ultimately granted amnesty by the Pierre Trudeau government. See Dominique Bernard, "La Commission d'enquête sur des opérations policières en territoire québécois: Portée réelle et limites du rapport Keable," MA thesis, Université du Québec à Montréal, 2008, 67.

71 In the end, Les Sinners decided not to participate in the event. JLQ-P-1994-0014-0106-A-1-A-2-L, September 3, 1972, recording of a performance at Petit Québec libre, JLC, Tenzier.

72 The pamphlet that contains this text was one of many documents that the QPP collected with the help of informants. See "Enlèvement et meurtre—Affaires Cross et Laporte (1970)," volume 2006-04-003/200, SQF, BAnQ.

73 JLQ-P-1994-0014-0106-A-1-A-2-L, September 3, 1972, recording of a performance at Petit Québec libre, JLC, Tenzier.

74 Patrice Beckerich, interview with author, February 17, 2012.

75 See draft of an undated essay by Yves Charbonneau on the history of the commune, YCF, CULSC.

76 "La critique est facile mais l'art est difficile," *Le P'tit Québec libre*, no. 5 (June 18, 1971): 1.

77 Patrice Beckerich, interview with author, February 17, 2012.

78 Cited in Maher, "Le Petit Québec libre," 2.

79 "Pour résoudre les contradictions au sein du Jazz libre du Québec," n.d., handwritten notes by Yves Charbonneau, YCF, CULSC.

## CHAPTER FIVE

1 Alain Richardson, "L'Amorce: Un nouvel endroit, une nouvelle conception," *Pop jeunesse* 2, no. 23 (December 1, 1973): 10.

2 Jean Préfontaine to the administrators of the Local Initiatives Program, January 20, 1973, JPF, CULSC.

3 "Pour résoudre les contradictions au sein du Jazz libre

du Québec," n.d., handwritten notes by Yves Charbonneau, YCF, CULSC.

4 Donat Valois, "Hué, Trudeau répond aux gars de Lapalme par un… 'souhait!,'" *La Presse*, February 3, 1971, G1.

5 Yves Bouliane, interview with author, February 11, 2012.

6 "Rapport financier et de progrès pour le Programme des initiatives locales," March 1, 1973, JPF, CULSC; JLQ-P-1994-0014-0120, April 22, 1972, recording of a performance in Pointe-Saint-Charles, JLC, Tenzier.

7 "Concerts-forums et questionnaire—Programme des initiatives locales," n.d., JPF, CULSC.

8 JLQ-P-1994-014-0121, 26 April 1972, recording of a performance in Montreal, JLC, Tenzier.

9 "Questionnaire—Programme des initiatives locales," n.d., JPF, CULSC.

10 Pierre Monat, interview with author, October 7, 2011.

11 JLQ-P-1994-0014-0099-A-1-A-2-L, February 4, 1973, recording of a concert in Montreal, JLC, Tenzier.

12 Jean Préfontaine to the administrators of the Local Initiatives Program, January 20, 1973, JPF, CULSC.

13 See Pierre Monat, *Y'a du dehors dedans*, Vidéographe, Montreal, 1973, video.

14 Jean Préfontaine to the administrators of the Local Initiatives Program, January 20, 1973, JPF, CULSC.

15 Ibid.

16 Yves Charbonneau did not explain how he understood and intended to implement "democratic socialism," but the organigram that accompanied his notes indicated his desire to see L'Amorce administered by a variety of committees, each of which would be overseen collectively by the members of Jazz Libre (then composed of Charbonneau, Jean Préfontaine, Jean-Guy Poirier, and Maurice Richard).

17 "Pour résoudre les contradictions au sein du Jazz libre du Québec," n.d., handwritten notes by Yves Charbonneau, YCF, CULSC.

18 Richardson, "L'Amorce," 10.

19 Charbonneau and Préfontaine, "Une nouvelle musique populaire," 7.

20 "Pour résoudre les contradictions au sein du Jazz libre du Québec," n.d., handwritten notes by Yves Charbonneau, YCF, CULSC.

21 "Propos sur la nouvelle musique 2," n.d., leaflet, YCF, CULSC.

22 "Propos sur la nouvelle musique 1," n.d., leaflet, YCF, CULSC.

23 Christiane Berthiaume, "La Relève-Québec mise en boîtes," *La Presse*, March 21, 1974, F1.

24 Charles Gagnon, *Pour le parti prolétarien* (Montreal: Équipe du journal, 1972), 8.

25 Pierre Vallières, *L'urgence de choisir* (Montreal: Parti pris, 1971), 87.

26 Yves Charbonneau, "Le Jazz libre est politique," *Le Jour*, June 1, 1974, V4.

27 Jean-Guy Poirier, interview with author, June 4, 2015.

28 "L'avventura socialista di Jazz libre du Québec," n.d., poster and program notes, JPF, CULSC.

29 Cited in Gilles Archambault, "Le Jazz libre dans ses meubles à l'Amorce, rue Saint-Paul," *Le Devoir*, August 9, 1973, 8.

30 Cited in Larue-Langlois, "Une musique jaillie de l'âme québécoise," 21.

31 See Raymond Gervais and Michel Di Torre, *Ce soir on improvise: Nouvelle musique au Québec*, Vidéographe, Montreal, 1974, video.

32 This is how Jean Préfontaine remembered Jazz Libre's position vis-à-vis the independence movement of the early 1970s. Jean Préfontaine to John Gilmore, December 4, 1985, JPF, CULSC.

33 Mathieu Léger, interview with author, February 21, 2012.

34 Yves Bouliane, interview with author, February 11, 2012.

35 Pierre Monat, interview with author, October 7, 2011.

36 "Rapport de l'enquêteur: Dossier 1611-no 74," January

21, 1975, Service de sécurité incendie de Montréal.

37 Gilmore, *Swinging in Paradise*, 350.

38 Kowch, "Radicals Met Near Barn Before Mounties Burned It," 4.

39 The name Gilles Choquette came up on numerous occasions during the interviews that I conducted for this book. Unfortunately, I was not able to locate—and meet with—this former commune dweller. His name did appear in the report that the authorities drafted following the fire at L'Amorce, but he was not explicitly listed as a suspect. "Notes de l'entrevue téléphonique avec Jean-Pierre Lemay (analyste, Section des incendies criminels du Service de police de la Ville de Montréal)," April 4, 1986, John Gilmore Fonds, CULSC.

40 See Jean Gagné and Serge Gagné, *Une semaine dans la vie de camarades*, Montreal, Cocagne, 1977, 16 mm.

## CONCLUSION

1 "Dixième édition du Festival international de jazz de Montréal," 1989, program, JLC, Tenzier.

2 Guy Thouin, interview with author, February 21, 2012. See also Alain Brunet, "La réunion du Jazz libre du Québec est annulée," *La Presse*, June 18, 1989, D2.

3 "Propos sur la nouvelle musique 1," n.d., leaflet, YCF, CULSC.

4 "Propos sur la nouvelle musique 2," n.d., leaflet, YCF, CULSC.

5 Patrice Beckerich, interview with author, February 17, 2012; Yves Bouliane, interview with author, February 11, 2012; Mathieu Léger, interview with author, February 21, 2012; Jacques Beaudoin, interview with author, December 9, 2015; Jean-Guy Poirier, interview with author, June 4, 2015; and Guy Thouin, interview with author, February 21, 2012.

6 Jean Derome, interview with author, May 31, 2012.

7 Jean Derome, "Le jazz à Montréal: D'un point de vue critique," *Moebius: Écriture/littérature*, no. 40 (1989): 26.

8 Jean Derome, interview with author, May 31, 2012.

9 Gabriela Coman, "Les manifestations de casseroles de 2012 au Québec, entre réparation politique et éveil civique," *Genèses* 119, no. 2 (2020): 209–23.

10 Jacques Attali, *Noise: The Political Economy of Music*, trans. Brian Massumi (Minneapolis: University of Minnesota Press, 2009), 6.

# Bibliography

(List of Select Secondary Sources)


Anderson, Iain. *This Is Our Music: Free Jazz, the Sixties, and American Culture*. Philadelphia: University of Pennsylvania Press, 2007.

Attali, Jacques. *Noise: The Political Economy of Music*. Translated by Brian Massumi. Minneapolis: University of Minnesota Press, 2009.

Austin, David. *Fear of a Black Nation: Race, Sex, and Security in Sixties Montreal*. Toronto: Between the Lines, 2013.

Backhouse, Constance. *Colour-Coded: A Legal History of Racism in Canada, 1900–1950*. Toronto: University of Toronto Press, 1999.

Belgrad, Daniel. *The Culture of Spontaneity: Improvisation and the Arts in Postwar America*. Chicago: University of Chicago Press, 1998.

Bernard, Dominique. "La Commission d'enquête sur des opérations policières en territoire québécois: Portée réelle et limites du rapport Keable." MA thesis, Université du Québec à Montréal, 2008.

Blais-Tremblay, Vanessa. "Gorgeous Girlies in Glittering Gyrations!: Capital érotique et danse jazz dans l'entre-deux-guerres québécois." *Recherches féministes* 32, no. 1 (2019): 89–109.

— . "Jazz, Gender, Historiography: A Case Study of the 'Golden Age' of Jazz in Montreal (1925–1955)." PhD dissertation, McGill University, 2018.

Bohlman, Philip V., and Goffredo Plastino, eds. *Jazz Worlds/World Jazz*. Chicago: University of Chicago Press, 2016.

Born, Georgina, Eric Lewis, and Will Straw, eds. *Improvisation and Social Aesthetics*. Durham: Duke University Press, 2017.

Campbell, Lara, Dominique Clément, and Gregory S. Kealey, eds. *Debating Dissent: Canada and the Sixties*. Toronto: University of Toronto Press, 2012.

Coates, Colin, ed. *Canadian Countercultures and the Environment*.

Calgary: University of Calgary Press, 2016.
Cotro, Vincent. *Chants libres: Le free jazz en France, 1960–1975.* Paris: Outre mesure, 1999.
Couture, Francine, ed. *Les arts visuels au Québec dans les années soixante. Tome 1: La reconnaissance de la modernité.* Montréal: VLB Éditeur, 1993.
— ed. *Les arts visuels au Québec dans les années soixante. Tome 2: L'éclatement du modernisme.* Montréal: VLB Éditeur, 1997.
De Carvalho, Anithe. *Art rebelle et contre-culture: Création collective underground au Québec.* Montreal: M Éditeur, 2015.
Drott, Eric. "Free Jazz and the French Critic." *Journal of the American Musicological Society* 61, no. 3 (2008): 541–81.
—. *Music and the Elusive Revolution: Cultural Politics and Political Culture in France, 1968–1981.* Berkeley: University of California Press, 2011.
Duchastel, Jules. "La contre-culture, une idéologie de l'apolitisme." In *La transformation du pouvoir au Québec. Actes du colloque de l'ACSALF (1979)*, edited by the Association canadienne des sociologues et anthropologues de langue française, 253–64. Montreal: Éditions Albert Saint-Martin, 1980.
Dumas, Carmel. *Montréal chaud/show: Chronique libre d'une explosion culturelle.* Montreal: Fides, 2008.
Dumont, Micheline. "La culture politique durant la Révolution tranquille: L'invisibilité des femmes dans *Cité libre* et l'*Action nationale.*" *Recherches féministes* 21, no. 2 (2008): 103–25.
Dupuis, Gilles, Karim Larose, Frédéric Rondeau, and Robert Schwartzwald, eds. *Avec ou sans* Parti pris: *Le legs d'une revue.* Montreal: Éditions Nota bene, 2018.
Elawani, Ralph. *C'est complet au royaume des morts: Emmanuel Cocke, le cascadeur de l'esprit.* Montreal: Tête première, 2014.
Felber, Andreas. *Die Wiener Free-Jazz-Avantgarde: Revolution im Hinterzimmer.* Vienne: Böhlau Verlag, 2005.
Fillion, Eric. "Jazz libre: 'Musique-action' ou la recherche d'une praxis révolutionnaire au Québec (1967–1975)." *Labour/Le Travail*, no. 77 (2016): 93–120.
–. "The New Quebec Man: Activism and Collective Improvisation

at Petit Québec libre, 1970–73." In *Making Men, Making History: Canadian Masculinities across Time and Place*, edited by Peter Gossage and Robert Rutherdale, 236–54. Vancouver: University of British Columbia Press, 2018.

– . "Le rock québécois débarque en France. *À soir on fait peur au monde, Tabarnac*, ou le retour par le rockumentaire." *Nouvelles Vues*, no. 16 (2015). www.nouvellesvues.ulaval.ca/index.php?id=2719.

Fischlin, Daniel, and Ajay Heble, eds. *The Other Side of Nowhere: Jazz, Improvisation, and Communities in Dialogue*. Middletown: Wesleyan University Press, 2004.

Fischlin, Daniel, Ajay Heble, and George Lipsitz. *The Fierce Urgency of Now: Improvisation, Rights, and the Ethics of Cocreation*. Durham: Duke University Press, 2013.

Fournier, Louis. *FLQ: Histoire d'un movement clandestin*. Montreal: Lanctôt Éditeur, 1998.

Gebhardt, Nicholas, and Tony Whyton, eds. *The Cultural Politics of Jazz Collectives: This Is Our Music*. New York: Routledge, 2015.

Gill, Louis. *Art, politique, révolution: Manifeste pour l'indépendance de l'art*. Montreal: M Éditeur, 2012.

Gilmore, John. *Swinging in Paradise: The Story of Jazz in Montreal*. Montreal: Véhicule Press, 1988.

– . *Who's Who of Jazz in Montreal: Ragtime to 1970*. Montreal: Véhicule Press, 1989.

Gossage, Peter, and J. I. Little. *An Illustrated History of Quebec: Tradition and Modernity*. Don Mills: Oxford University Press, 2013.

Heble, Ajay. *Landing on the Wrong Note: Jazz, Dissonance, and Critical Practice*. New York: Routledge, 2000.

Heble, Ajay, and Rob Wallace, eds. *People Get Ready: The Future of Jazz Is Now*. Durham: Duke University Press, 2013.

Heffley, Mike. *Northern Sun/Southern Moon: Europe's Reinvention of Jazz*. London: Yale University Press, 2005.

Jago, Marian. *Live at the Cellar: Vancouver's Iconic Jazz Club and the Canadian Co-operative Jazz Scene in the 1950s and '60s*. Vancouver: University of British Columbia Press, 2018.

Jezo-Vannier, Steven. *San Francisco: L'utopie libertaire des sixties.* Paris: Le mot et le reste, 2010.

Jost, Ekkehard. *Free Jazz.* New York: Da Capo, 1994.

Lafleur, Guillaume. *Pratiques minoritaires: Fragments d'une histoire méconnue du cinéma québécois (1937–1973).* Montreal: Nota bene, 2015.

Lanthier, Stéphanie. "L'impossible réciprocité des rapports politiques et idéologiques entre le nationalisme radical et le féminisme radical au Québec, 1961–1972." MA thesis, Université de Sherbrooke, 1998.

La Rochelle, Réal. "Arcand, Denys (1941– )." In *Dictionnaire de la censure au Québec*, edited by Pierre Hébert, Yves Lever, and Kenneth Landry, 45–50. Montreal: Fides, 2006.

Larose, Karim, and Frédéric Rondeau, eds. *La contre-culture au Québec.* Montreal: Presses de l'Université de Montréal, 2016.

Lee, David. "Outside the Empire: Improvised Music in Toronto, 1960–1985." PhD dissertation, University of Guelph, 2017.

Lewis, George. *A Power Stronger than Itself: The AACM and Amercan Experimental Music.* Chicago: University of Chicago Press, 2008.

Linteau, Paul-André, René Durocher, Jean-Claude Robert, and François Ricard. *Histoire du Québec contemporain. Tome II: Le Québec depuis 1930.* Montreal: Boréal, 1989.

Major, Robert. *Parti pris: Idéologies et littérature.* Montreal: Cahiers du Québec/Hurtubise HMH, 1979.

Marrelli, Nancy. *Burgundy Jazz: Little Burgundy and the Story of Montreal Jazz.* Montreal: Véhicule Press, 2013.

Maynard, Robyn. *Policing Black Lives: State Violence in Canada from Slavery to the Present.* Halifax: Fernwood Publishing, 2017.

McKay, George. *Circular Breathing: The Cultural Politics of Jazz in Britain.* Durham: Duke University Press, 2005.

Miller, Mark. *Jazz in Canada: Fourteen Lives.* Toronto: University of Toronto Press, 1982.

–. *The Miller Companion to Jazz in Canada and Canadians in Jazz.* Toronto: Mercury Press, 2001.

–. *Such Melodious Racket: The Lost History of Jazz in Canada, 1914–1949.* Toronto: Mercury Press, 1997.

Mills, Sean. "Democracy in Music: Louis Metcalf and Montreal's Jazz History." *Canadian Historical Review* 100, no. 3 (2019): 351–72.

– . *The Empire Within: Postcolonial Thought and Political Activism in Sixties Montreal*. Montreal: McGill-Queen's University Press, 2010.

Monson, Ingrid. *Freedom Sounds: Civil Rights Call Out to Jazz and Africa*. New York: Oxford University Press, 2007.

– . *Saying Something: Jazz Improvisation and Interaction*. Chicago: University of Chicago Press, 1996.

Moore, Hilary. *Inside British Jazz: Crossing Borders of Race, Nation, and Class*. Aldershot: Ashgate Publishing, 2007.

Mullen, Bill V. *Afro-Orientalism*. Minneapolis: University of Minnesota Press, 2004.

O'Leary, Véronique, and Louise Toupin, eds. *Québécoises deboutte! Tome 1*. Montreal: Remue-ménage, 1982.

Palaeologu, M. Athena, ed. *The Sixties in Canada: A Turbulent and Creative Decade*. Montreal: Black Rose Books, 2009.

Palmer, Bryan D. *Canada's 1960s: The Ironies of Identity in a Rebellious Era*. Toronto: University of Toronto Press, 2009.

Perone, James E. *Music of the Counterculture Era*. Westport: Greenwood Press, 2004.

Robert, Frédéric, and Armand Hage. *Révoltes et utopies: La contre-culture américaine dans les années 1960*. Rennes: Presses universitaires de Rennes, 2011.

Rouillard, Jacques. *Le syndicalisme québécois*. Montreal: Boréal, 2004.

Roy, Bruno. *L'Osstidcho ou le désordre libérateur*. Montreal: XYZ, 2008.

Sklower, Jedediah. *Free Jazz, la catastrophe féconde: Une histoire du monde éclaté du jazz en France (1960–1982)*. Paris: L'Harmattan, 2006.

– . "Rebel with the Wrong Cause. Albert Ayler et la signification du free jazz en France (1959–1971)." *Volume!* 6, nos. 1–2 (2008): 193–219.

Vacante, Jeffery. "Quebec Manhood in Historical Perspective." In *Canadian Men and Masculinities: Historical and Contemporary*

*Perspectives*, edited by Christopher J. Greig and Wayne J. Martino, 23–41. Toronto: Canadian Scholars' Press, 2012.

Vachon, Marc. *L'arpenteur de la ville: L'utopie urbaine situationniste et Patrick Straram*. Montreal: Triptyque, 2003.

Vincent, Rickey. *Party Music: The Inside Story of the Black Panthers' Band and How Black Power Transformed Soul Music*. Chicago: Lawrence Hill Books, 2013.

Warren, Jean-Philippe. *Ils voulaient changer le monde: Le militantisme marxiste-léniniste au Québec*. Montreal: VLB Éditeur, 2007.

– . *Une douce anarchie: Les années 68 au Québec*. Montreal: Boréal, 2008.

– . "Un parti pris sexuel: Sexualité et masculinité dans la revue *Parti pris*." *Globe: Revue internationale d'études québécoises* 12, no. 2 (2009): 129–57.

Warren, Jean-Philippe, and Andrée Fortin. *Pratiques et discours de la contre-culture au Québec*. Quebec City: Septentrion, 2015.

Whiteley, Sheila, and Jedediah Sklower, eds. *Countercultures and Popular Music*. London: Routledge, 2014.

Williams, Dorothy W. *The Road to Now: A History of Blacks in Montreal*. Montreal: Véhicule Press, 1997.

# Index


African Americans
  activists, connections to, 53, 96
  analogy to, 23, 35, 51–54, 73, 94, 114, 134, 163
  musicians, exposure to, 34–35, 38, 42
Ali, Rashied, 34
*américanité*, 60, 71, 98
anti-capitalism, 50, 81, 146
  "anti-capitalist pop festival" (*See under* festivals)
  and anti-imperialism, 20–21, 26, 49, 94, 114, 128, 134, 137, 147
anti-colonialism, 20–21, 51, 53
  decolonization
    "decolonizing socialism" in Quebec, 17, 25, 47, 49, 51, 161–62, 182n6 (See also *Parti Pris*; Straram, Patrick)
    international contexts, 53, 119, 134, 161–62
  Quebec as colony, 17, 20–21, 23, 53, 94, 98, 114, 119, 150
Armstrong, Mike, 29–30, 36. *See also* Barrel, The; Jazz Workshop
arson, 129, 156–57
Association des Patriotes Vietnamiens de Montréal, 128, 151. *See also* Vietnam, War in
Association Espagnole
  association with *Parti Pris*, 54–55
  base for Jazz Libre, 27, 57–58, 61, 84, 104, 106, 119, 140–41
  *L'art de manger* event, 88
  site of La Casanous, 149
Association Socialiste pour l'Indépendance du Québec, 17. *See also* Roy, Raoul
Atelier de Musique Expérimentale, 164–65
Automatism, 25, 31–32, 35, 47–48, 88
Ayler, Albert, 18–19, 29, 36

Bachand, François Mario, 112. *See also* FLQ
Balcer, Lise, 119, 123–25
Barash, Lucie, 57, 148
Baron Filip. *See* Gingras, Philippe
Barrel, The, 29, 34–37, 42–43, 56, 88, 106, 149
Basile, Jean (alias Pénélope), 107, 126
Bastiaan, Peter, 148
Beaudoin, Jacques, 140, 163
Beckerich, Patrice, 116–17, 131, 133, 162
Black Bottom, 145
Black Panther Party, 20, 53, 104, 119, 128
Bley, Paul, 38
Borduas, Paul-Émile, 31
Borremans, Guy, 44, 50, 55
Boudreau, Walter, 41–42, 72, 75–82, 100
Bouliane, Yves, 140–41, 143, 155, 162, 164

Brégent, Michel-Georges, 148
Brown, Marion, 51

Casseroles (protest), 166–67
Césaire, Aimé, 53. *See also* négritude
Chamberland, Paul, 46–48, 74–75
*chansonniers,* 22, 59–60. *See also* folk music
Chantraine, Pol, 102, 104
Charbonneau, Yves. *See* Jazz Libre
Charlebois, Robert
  and American counterculture, 58–60 (*See also* counterculture)
  influence of, 95, 97–98, 159
  *Osstidcho* concerts, 15, 61–66, 69–71, 75, 80, 83–84, 91
  Paris concerts, 15, 67–70, 151
  recordings, 58–59, 66–67, 70
Chiasson, Richard, 34
Choquette, Gilles, 119, 201n39
civil rights movement, 20, 40, 77
Cocke, Emmanuel, 29–30, 37–38, 56, 72, 89
Coleman, Ornette, 18–19, 38
Colonie Artistique de Val-David. *See under* Jazz Libre
Coltrane, John, 44, 72
communes. *See under* Jazz Libre: Colonie Artistique de Val-David; Petit Québec Libre
concert forums. *See under* Jazz Libre
counterculture
  Charlebois and, 59–60, 97
  commercialism as "theft of," 98, 101
  left-wing independence movement and, 45, 77–78, 133, 164
  relationship of Jazz Libre to, 28, 35, 58, 80, 97
  youth and, 18, 25, 77–78, 84, 95–96, 102–3, 126, 130–33, 164

Dansereau, Fernand, 89–90
Davis, Miles, 35, 38, 72
Debord, Guy, 49, 85. *See also* situationism
Derome, Jean, 148, 165
Deschamps, Yvon, 15, 60, 63–64, 69
Désormeaux, Jacques, 119
Di Torre, Michel, 164
diaspora
  African, 20, 23, 25, 51–53, 134 (*See also* African Americans; Montreal: Black community)
Dionne, Vincent, 164
Dionysos, 98, 102, 105, 130
drugs
  recreational use, 96, 101–5, 127, 130–31
Duguay, Raôul, 71–76, 148
Dupuis, Diane, 93, 110

En Lutte!, 149, 161
Ensemble de Musique Improvisée de Montréal, 165
Expo 67, 16–17, 36–37
  and counterculture, 58
  and Jean Drapeau's "clean-up campaign," 40

effects on musicians, 41
jazz at Youth Pavillion, 41, 72, 85, 100

Fanon, Frantz, 44, 53
feminism, 108, 123–25, 162
festivals
"anti-capitalist pop festival," 102–6, 126, 130–32, 143
Autostade, 98
Autunno Musicale, 151–52
Francofolies, 166
Montreal International Jazz Festival, 159–60
Rencontre Internationale de la Contre-Culture, 158
Toronto Pop Festival, 70
Woodstock Pop Festival (Manseau), 101, 103, 105, 153
films
at Petit Québec Libre, 111
Fusion des Arts film festivals, 87
Jazz Libre soundtracks, 153–54
jazz-inspired, 44–45
Montreal International Film Festival, 85
in multimedia performance, 74
of Charlebois Paris concerts, 68–69
of concert forums, 89–90, 142–43
Foisy, Fernand, 115
folk music, 22, 36, 58–60, 100, 145, 165
folklore, 165
Forestier, Louise, 15, 60–70
recordings, 66–67, 70
France, 32, 50–51, 66–67, 151
Paris, 32, 51, 112, 117, 152
Charlebois concerts, 15, 67–68, 81
free jazz
as African American music, 19–20 (*See also under* African Americans: appropriation from)
as revolutionary practice/praxis, 15, 19–21, 25, 27–28, 62, 80, 84, 106, 109, 111–12, 135, 146–47, 161 (*See also* Jazz Libre: music action)
as alienating, 88, 93–94, 133
Jazz Libre on, 87–88, 100–1, 109, 146
origins, 18–19
reception in France, 20, 51 (*See also* Charlebois, Robert; France)
reception in Quebec, 34, 36–39, 43–56 (See also under *Parti pris;* Straram, Patrick)
Front de Libération du Québec (FLQ)
connections to Jazz Libre (*See under* Jazz Libre)
October Crisis, 17, 108, 117–19, 121, 149
*See also* Gagnon, Charles; Vallières, Pierre
Fusion des Arts, 84–88, 147

Gagnon, Bernard, 164
Gagnon, Charles, 53, 149

imprisonment, 62, 87 (*See also* Vallières, Pierre)
*See also* FLQ
Gauvreau, Claude, 32, 62, 153–54
Gervais, Raymond, 164
Gingras, Philippe (alias Baron Filip), 88, 158
Graham, Françoise, 89–90
Greenwich, Sonny, 38, 100
Groulx, Gilles, 44, 50, 55

Highbloom, Bryan, 148, 164
hippies, 59, 77, 80, 97, 102, 108, 130
Honsinger, Tristan, 138, 148
Howard, Noah, 34, 51
Hubbard, Freddie, 35

imperialism, 114
American, 17, 49, 59
anti-imperialism, 17, 20–26, 49, 51, 94, 128, 137, 147
independence
and art, 31, 164
leftist independence movement, 18, 21, 23, 25, 28, 42, 45–49, 51–53, 63, 106, 111–12, 115, 118, 121, 123, 126, 133, 146, 161–63
schism within, 135, 137, 149–50, 155
*See also* separatism
Italy, 151–53

Jardin des glaces, 145
Jazz Libre
audiences, 28, 37–38
intentions for, 22–23, 41, 55–56, 60–61, 71, 74–75, 146
reception, 57, 64–70, 83–91, 93–95, 100–1, 105, 132–35, 141–44, 152–54, 163
Colonie Artistique de Val-David, 24, 27, 84, 99–109, 112, 119, 126, 139, 145, 162
community opposition to, 103–4
concert forums, 83–84
at schools, 90–94, 100, 127, 133, 136
under LIP, 139, 142–44, 150
connections to FLQ, 18, 23, 54, 62, 102, 106, 108–9, 112–15, 119–23, 127, 129
dissolution, 156–58
formation, 29–35
on free jazz, 87–88, 100–1, 109, 146
influences (*See* African Americans: musicians, exposure to; *Parti pris;* Straram, Patrick)
in Italy, 151–153
as Jazz Lib' du Kebek, 158
at Jazz Workshop, 29–30, 36, 36–37, 37–38, 42, 56
L'Amorce, 24, 27, 162
activities, 146–51, 153
establishment, 136–38, 144
fire, 156–57
*Le P'tit Québec libre,* 114,

122–24, 127
with L'Infonie, 58, 75–84, 95, 97, 138, 159
music action
as praxis, 24, 26, 43, 57, 81, 83–84, 87, 108, 112, 134, 137, 143, 154, 161, 163
Petit Québec Libre, 18, 107–35, 137, 143, 146, 151, 157, 162
recordings, 11–12, 65–67, 70, 81, 115
as Rock Libre, 69–70
with Robert Charlebois
*Osstidcho* concerts, 15, 61–66, 69–71, 75, 80, 83–84, 91
Paris concerts, 15, 67–70, 151
*See also* members Beaudoin, Jacques; Beckerich, Patrice; Bouliane, Yves; Charbonneau, Yves; Chiasson, Richard; Honsinger, Tristan; Johnston, Gaby; Léger, Mathieu; Lepage, Cyril; Martineau, Jean; Poirier, Jean-Guy; Préfontaine, Jean; Richard, Maurice (musician); Thouin, Guy; Virgil, Curly
Jazz Workshop, 29–30, 36–37, 42, 56
Johnston, Gaby, 76, 79, 141

Keable Commission, 129–30, 157
La Casanous, 149. *See also* Association Espagnole
La Grande Passe, 148–49, 158
La Révolution Française, 98
Lacroix, Richard, 84, 86, 89
L'Amorce. *See under* Jazz Libre
Lapalme guys, 116, 133, 138, 195n30
Latraverse, Guy, 69–70
Lefebvre, Henri, 49–50, 85
Lefebvre, Jean Pierre, 44, 50
leftism. *See* Marxism; socialism
Léger, Mathieu, 153, 162
Lemoyne, Serge, 74, 88, 148
L'Engrenage. *See under* theatre: Théâtre des Travailleurs
Lepage, Cyril, 100–101, 139
Lepage, Robert M., 140, 164
Leriche, Robert, 148, 165
Les Champignons, 130
Les Sinners, 130
Levant (band), 105
*Liberté*, 43, 46, 50
L'Infonie, 58, 75–84, 95, 97, 138, 159
recordings, 78–79
Local Initiatives Program, 136–38, 141–46, 148–50
*Logos*, 95, 98
London Records of Canada, 65, 159
Los Quinchamali, 130

Madore, Michel, 158
Maheu, Pierre, 46–48
*Mainmise*, 95, 98, 126
Major, André, 46–47
Maltais, Marcella, 32
Manseau. *See under* festivals
Maple Spring, 166
Martineau, Jean, 140
Marxism, 87, 114, 150, 168

tendencies
Maoism, 23, 108, 120, 135, 150, 161
Marxist-Leninism, 21, 108, 120, 135, 149–50, 154–56, 161
Trotskyism, 120, 146
Mayr, Albert, 151
McHugh, Freddy, 100
Memmi, Albert, 53
Metcalf, Louis, 39
Monat, Pierre, 142, 145, 155
Monfette, Claudine (alias Mouffe), 15, 60, 63, 69
Montreal
Black community, 39–40, 53–54, 119
neighbourhoods, 30, 39–40, 54, 91, 113, 135–36, 141, 145, 148–49, 151, 156
Mouffe. *See* Monfette, Claudine
Murray, Sunny, 18–19, 29, 34, 36, 51
music action. *See under* Jazz Libre

Nadeau, Pierre, 65, 90, 159
nationalism
Black, 20
Quebec (*See* independence; separatism)
and socialism, 28, 150, 154–55 (*See also* socialism)
négritude, 53, 73
Nouvelles Frontières, 102, 105

O'Cannabis, 105, 130
October Crisis. *See under* FLQ
*Osstidcho. See under* Charlebois, Robert

*Parti pris*
ideology, 17, 46–55, 72–75, 81, 85, 94, 115, 119–20, 147, 162
and jazz, 21, 23–24, 46, 49–54, 72–75, 81, 147
Parti Québécois, 135, 149–50, 155, 160, 165–66
Patapalace, 145
Pathografik, 145
Perron, Jacques, 61, 69
Peterson, Oscar, 39
Petit Québec Libre. *See under* Jazz Libre
*Poèmes et chansons de la résistance,* 62–63, 65
Poirier, Jean-Guy, 139–40, 151–53
police
agent provocateurs, 132, 157
harassment, 104, 127
raids, 108
repression, 122, 135, 149
violence, 77, 119
*See also* Royal Canadian Mounted Police; Sûreté du Quebec
Pop music, 35, 41, 59–60, 70, 98, 100–105, 117, 131
Préfontaine, Jean. *See* Jazz Libre
Préfontaine, Yves, 43
Psychedelia, 57–58, 78–79, 92, 140

Quebec
Communist Party, 120, 195n35 (*See also*

Marxism)
Liberal Party, 16, 161
Local Initiatives Program, 136–38, 141–46, 148–50
Ministry of Cultural Affairs, 91, 165
Provincial Police (*See* Sûreté du Quebec)
referenda, 160, 165–66
*See also* independence; Montreal; nationalism; separatism
*québécité,* 60, 71, 94
*québécitude,* 23. *See also* African Americans, analogy to; négritude
Quiet Revolution, 25, 27, 30, 48–49, 85–86

racism
against Black musicians, 39, 43
denial of, 53
protest against, 119
racial segregation, 20
*See also under* African Americans
Radio-Canada, 37, 43, 75, 89–90, 118, 140
Radio-Canada International, 65, 159
Rassemblement pour l'Indépendance Nationale, 17, 118–19
referenda, 160, 165–66
*Refus global,* 31, 47. *See also* Automatism
Richard, Maurice (musician)
departure from Jazz Libre, 81, 109, 112
recruitment to Jazz Libre, 33
*See also* Jazz Libre
Riley, Terry, 78
Riopelle, Jean-Paul, 32
Robillard, Yves, 84–85
rock music, 40, 57–82, 98, 130, 132, 140, 165
Rollins, Sonny, 38
Rose, Paul, 106, 108, 118–20, 124. *See also* FLQ; October Crisis
Rossignol, Iolande, 89–90
Roy, Raoul, 17, 49. *See also* Association Socialiste pour l'Indépendance du Québec
Royal Canadian Mounted Police, 108, 121, 127–28, 138, 157
arson at Petit Québec Libre, 129, 135, 157
surveillance, 18, 101, 129, 137

Saint-Jacques, Pierre, 165
Saint-Jean-Baptiste Day
21 to 24 events (1968), 88–89
fire at L'Amorce (1974), 156–57
parade (1968), 118
separatism, 23, 162
indépendantistes, 43
sovereignty-association, 135, 160–61 (*See also* Parti Québécois)
*See also* independence; nationalism
sexism, 123–24, 162
Shepp, Archie, 18–20, 29, 36
Shorter, Alan, 51

Silva, Alan, 51
Simard, Francis, 106, 108, 118–19. *See also* FLQ; October Crisis
Sir George Williams University (Concordia)
  occupation, 118
situationism, 25, 45, 49, 142 *See also* Debord, Guy
Smack (band), 105
socialism
  communes (*See under* Jazz Libre: Colonie Artistique de Val-David; Petit Québec Libre)
  "decolonizing socialism," 17, 25, 47, 49, 51, 161–62, 182n6 (See also *Parti pris;* Straram, Patrick)
  and independence movement (*See under* independence)
Spanier, Herbie, 38
Straram, Patrick
  influence on Jazz Libre, 21–22, 45–46, 75, 84, 147
  theorizing on jazz, 49–55, 72–73, 147
  See also *Parti Pris*
strikes, 114, 116, 133
students, 108, 118–19, 126–27, 150, 166
Sullivan, Françoise, 32
Sun Ra, 38, 97
Sûreté du Quebec, 102–4, 126–28, 137
surveillance. *See under* Royal Canadian Mounted Police; Sûreté du Quebec
swing music, 33, 39, 72

Taylor, Cecil, 18–19, 65
Technique d'Action Sociale, 84, 87, 147. *See also* Fusion des Arts
terrorism, 17–18, 62, 108, 118, 120, 122, 129, 164
  as metaphor, 42, 56, 160
"The Internationale," 151–53, 158, 163
theatre
  Théâtre de Quat'sous, 60, 63–64, 91
  Théâtre des Travailleurs, 116–17, 148
  Théâtre Radical du Québec, 111
Thomas, René, 38, 44
Thouin, Guy
  departure from Jazz Libre, 81–82
  recruitment to Jazz Libre, 32–33
  *See also* Jazz Libre
Trois Points Virgule, 148

unions, 107–8, 114–17, 133, 138, 149
universities, 91, 119, 126–27, 150–51, 159
utopianism, 18, 78, 86, 102

Vaillancourt, Serge, 158
Val-David. *See under* Jazz Libre: Colonie Artistique de Val-David
Vallières, Pierre
  imprisonment, 62, 87 (*See also* Gagnon, Charles)

*La Claque*, editor of, 102
and Parti Quebecois, 135, 149–50
on Quebec as colony, 17, 21, 53
*White Niggers of America*, 17, 23, 52, 94–95, 120, 162
*See also* FLQ
Valois, Jacques, 41, 79, 92, 100, 141
Vietnam, War in
as political inspiration, 119–20, 161
draft dodgers, 138
protest against, 65, 72, 74, 77, 96
Virgil, Curly, 101–2, 139

War Measures Act, 118, 138
Waterlot, Daniel, 120, 195n35
Weather Underground, 128
working class
as audience, 105, 112–16, 133–36, 144–45, 150–51, 162
at Petit Québec Libre, 110, 133–36, 150

yéyé, 59–60
Young Lords, 128, 164
youth
counterculture, 18, 25, 77–78, 84, 95–96, 102–3, 126, 130–33, 164
students, 108, 118–19, 126–27, 150, 166

Zirmate, 74–75, 88